BEYOND THE DANCE

CHAN HON GOH

BEYOND THE DANCE

A Ballerina's Life

with Cary Fagan

TUNDRA BOOKS

Published in Canada by Tundra Books,
481 University Avenue, Toronto, Ontario M5G 2E9

Published in the United States by Tundra Books of Northern New York,
P.O. Box 1030, Plattsburgh, New York 12901

Library of Congress Control Number: 2002101724

National Library of Canada Cataloguing in Publication Data

Goh, Chan Hon
Beyond the dance: a ballerina's life

ISBN 0-88776-596-3

1. Goh, Chan Hon. 2. National Ballet of Canada–Biography.
3. Ballerinas–Canada–Biography. I. Fagan, Cary II. Title

GV1785.G613A3 2002   792.8'092   C2002-900783-6

We acknowledge the support of the Canada Council for the Arts and
the Ontario Arts Council for our publishing program.

We acknowledge the financial support of the Government of Canada through
the Book Publishing Industry Development Program for our publishing activities.

Design: Kong Njo

Printed and bound in Canada

1 2 3 4 5 6   07 06 05 04 03 02

For my parents, Choo Chiat and Lin Yee,

my constant source of strength and love.

– Chan Hon Goh

With Aleksandar Antonijevic in "Diamonds" from George Balanchine's Jewels.

CONTENTS

✳

DANCING FOR A QUEEN

My debut as the Swan Queen, Odette, with Robert Tewsley in Erik Bruhn's production of Swan Lake *(with the Royal Danish Ballet, I danced the Peter Martins version).*

T he Royal Danish Ballet is one of the greatest companies of the world. So naturally I was thrilled to be asked to dance with them as a guest artist during the 250th anniversary year of The Royal Theatre in Copenhagen.

The ballet was *Swan Lake*, which is not only the most popular ballet of all time but also one of the most difficult and exhausting for any ballerina to perform. At the National Ballet of Canada, I had just ended our own tiring season and had only seven days to prepare, with a partner – Johan Kobborg – who was to make his debut as Prince Siegfried. I arrived in Copenhagen on a chilly March day and began unpacking my things in the hotel room. Instead of happy expectation, I was feeling strangely low, and as I took out each item I felt a little more lonely, a little more homesick, a little more anxious. I was twenty-eight years old and married, but I felt almost like a child again, sure that I would not be liked, that I would not fit in. I had to tell myself: *You have been a principal dancer for four years. You've just danced* Romeo and Juliet *to critical acclaim. You are going to dance well. They are going to like you.*

The principal ballerina in *Swan Lake* must perform two roles – the beautiful White Swan, named Odette, and the dangerous temptress Odile, the Black Swan. In the rehearsal studio, the company's associate director helped teach me the steps, for this *Swan Lake* was the version choreographed by Peter Martins of the New York City Ballet, and it was different from the ones I had danced before. So much more of it had to be danced up on pointe that my toes became badly blistered from practicing. Johan was a new partner for me – a dancer needs to absolutely trust her partner – and we did not meet until the first day of rehearsal. So although the rehearsals were going well enough, I could not help feeling tremendous anxiety. One morning, having breakfast alone in the hotel and looking at the happy couples and families around me, again I felt overwhelmed with loneliness and the childlike desire to be protected by my parents who were thousands of miles away, back in Vancouver. Leaving my breakfast, I hurried back to my room and started to cry. I cried for a good long while, and when I felt better I picked up my bag and headed to the theater for morning class.

The night of the first performance arrived. Waiting for my first entrance, I stood in the wings of the theater, jumping up and down to keep warm so that my muscles would not seize up. The first entrance in *Swan Lake* is the hardest – the ballerina has to "emerge" from the lake, expressing her enchanted swan form through the interpretation of the steps. I heard my music, and saw Johan already on stage and deeply into the role, and I knew it would be all right.

And it *was* all right, at least until the third act. Then came the infamous moment when, as the Black Swan Odile, I had to execute the thirty-two fouettés. A fouetté is a very quick spin in which the working leg whips around to create momentum as the supporting foot moves onto pointe for the turn, then down flat, and onto pointe again. Fouettés are done repeatedly, keeping the dancer whirling on the spot. I had to perform this bravura display after already being fatigued from the previous variation. I began the fouettés on the unfamiliar stage, and they were going well enough for me to throw in some "doubles" for show, when

Backstage with Johan Kobborg, Johnny Eliasen (coach), and Maina Gielgud (artistic director).

my foot hit a ridge on the stage floor, possibly the edge of a trap door used for operas. Almost losing my rhythm, I was filled with sudden terror. Yet I still had twenty more turns to go.

Calm down, calm down.

I managed to rescue the fouettés and get through the rest of the ballet, although I feared that I wouldn't. The only other glitch occurred when I was supposed to turn and meet the prince face to face, only to discover that he was way upstage. I literally had to bolt to reach him in time. What gave me strength to the end was looking in Johan's eyes and seeing how much emotion he felt as the prince, making my Odette and Odile come alive. I myself was learning the deeper truth that great dance was not simply about doing the steps perfectly.

The experience of appearing at the Royal Danish Ballet, which had frightened me so much at the start, turned out to be one of the highlights of my career. The reviews in the Danish newspapers were wonderful and with each performance my confidence grew. To my delight, the Queen of Denmark came to the last show. On that night my only problem was remembering to bow first to the Queen's box during the curtain calls. Beside me, Johan kept having to remind me by whispering in my ear.

CHAPTER I

BEARS ARE SHAKING MY BED

The bears were all around the bed, standing in their hunched-over, hulking way. And with their great paws they were shaking the bed, and me in it. Shaking, shaking. But I wasn't afraid, because I felt in their soft bear faces and their warm breath and their dark eyes that they didn't mean me any harm. . . .

"Da Hong, get up! We have to get out of here!" My mother's voice. How reluctantly I opened my eyes, making the bears disappear. Now my mother leaned over me looking frantic. Somehow the bed was still shaking. What time was it? Outside, it was still dark, not yet time for my grade-one class, so why was my mother bothering me?

"Da Hong, it's an earthquake, we've got to hurry."

I got out of bed and let her lead me to the stairs where a stream of people, the neighbors in our building, were already moving down. Everyone was still wearing pajamas, blinking away sleep, faces pale and fearful. The pain of missing my father came back to me. He was so far away, on the other side of the world, and so he could not help us. I tried

As Cinderella en route to the Royal Ball. The fairy tales my father told me would eventually come true.

Age six, with my one and only doll, a rare toy.

to distract myself by imagining what Daddy was doing now, in his new strange country called Canada. But I couldn't picture anything.

We had said good-bye to my father a few months before. It was winter and he wore his heavy coat and wool scarf as he stood on the tarmac beside the stairs up to the airplane. He gave me a hug, and told me to be good in every way and that he would see me soon. But I knew that my mother and I hadn't received permission to leave China. I watched him walk up the stairs and go through the airplane door, and then there he was at the little window waving to us. I was seven years old and, strangely enough, I didn't cry but felt a terrible emptiness inside me.

While I was close to both my parents, I had always felt a special bond with my father. Maybe it was because my mother had rheumatoid arthritis and couldn't participate in games or carry me because of the pain. It was Dad who got down on his hands and knees to play. Because he had

Age six, having just seen the musical The Red Lantern.

lived in Singapore and even London, England, he had a knowledge of Western ways that was very rare in China, and he sometimes fixed my hair like the stars in American and British movies he had seen. The lady who opened the gates of our apartment complex and the other residents there would say jokingly, "Oh, she looks like a little foreign girl." At other times he would tell me fairy tales like *Sleeping Beauty* or *Cinderella*, although he sometimes got the stories mixed up because such tales had become forbidden in China and he hadn't heard them in years. Still, it made me feel special to know that my father had been to the West.

My mother and I returned from the airport to our apartment in the city. Inside, everything was the same – the furniture, the cups and dishes on the table – but everything was different. Now I felt like crying but I knew that it would upset my mother even more, so I managed to stop myself.

The next day my father phoned from Hong Kong where he was staying with a cousin before going on to Canada. Nobody in the

The winter before the earthquake, me, my maternal grandmother Lau Lau, and my cousin Ping.

apartment complex had a private phone – in China we had almost no private luxuries – so we had to use the one in the reception room. And right there in that place where other residents were coming and going my mother and I started to cry for the first time.

The earthquake of July 28, 1976, had a magnitude of 8.2 and was the deadliest of the century. Most of the people killed lived in or near Tianjin, on the eastern coast, at the center of the earthquake. Still, in Beijing there was much damage and many buildings were no longer safe, including the complex where my family lived with the other dancers of the Central Ballet of China. We had to sleep in a tent in one of the public parks. For a washroom we had to use an outhouse that was dirty and crawling with insects. How I hated to go in there! After a couple of weeks, my grandmother decided it would be better for us to move to the yard next to her house.

Months later, we returned to our apartment. My mother and I had become closer now that we were alone, and we shared the common hope of leaving China to see my father again. She told me not to talk with the other kids in school about missing him or leaving China, in case they became resentful or considered me anti-Chinese. So I kept my empty feeling — my deep well of loneliness — to myself. Oddly, this feeling sometimes comes back to me even now, so many years later, when I am on tour and far away from the securities of home. Alone in a strange hotel room, unsure of what to expect from the theater or the audience — or even my fellow dancers if I am making a guest performance — I feel anxious and fearful. It is then that my childhood emotions flood back and for a moment I feel like that small girl again, pining for her father.

CHAPTER 2

%

DANCING FOR THE REVOLUTION

In 1999, I was
a special guest
with the National
Ballet of China
on its fortieth
anniversary.
The Revolutionary
ballet The Red
Detachment
of Women
was performed
in excerpt.

Our family is from China. My mother, Lin Yee, was born and raised in Beijing. But my father, Choo Chiat Goh, grew up on the island of Singapore, the fortunate son of a successful businessman and factory owner. He also grew up in a most unusual family structure, for my father had not one but two mothers. As a young man his father (my grandfather) fell in love with a Malaysian woman and married her in a secret and unofficial ceremony. They had one child before my grandfather's family pressured him into marrying a Chinese woman. He did so, but after the wedding he told his new wife about the first, and that his Malaysian wife would be living with them. And so they all made a life together in remarkable harmony. My father, the fifth of the nine children my grandfather's second wife had, was close not only to his birth mother but to his other mother as well, who took him under her wing and with whom he had a special bond.

That my father wanted to be an artist — of all things, a ballet dancer — was shocking to my grandfather, who considered a career in the arts far too insecure and only for people who weren't smart enough to go

· 19 ·

into business. But Choo Chiat had seen the ballet movie *The Red Shoes* and was so passionate and insistent that his father gave in and let him study dance, first in Singapore and then, while still very young, at the famous Royal Ballet School in London, England. My father's older sister Soo Nee was already studying there, so he had someone to keep an eye on him.

Naturally talented and totally devoted to his art, my father impressed Harold Turner of the Royal Ballet School and later Nadine Legat, his well-known teachers in London. At sixteen, he was invited to turn professional and join the celebrated London Festival Ballet. But my father, subjecting himself to the highest standards, felt that he wasn't ready. He had read in the newspapers that the Soviet Union was sending the great ballet master, Pyotr Gusiev (who was also the teacher of the young Rudolf Nureyev), to teach in Beijing. In London, Father had been impressed by the Russian dance companies most of all and he immediately decided to go to China so that he might study with Gusiev. And there was something else drawing him too: a longing to see the country of his ancestors.

Choo Chiat returned from London to Singapore to speak with his parents about the idea. Go to China! His parents were aghast. China had a hard-line Communist government headed by Chairman Mao Zedong. People in China, his father said, did not have enough to eat, or decent clothes to wear. Besides, they did not have the same freedoms that people in the West had. To make matters worse, if Choo Chiat did not return from China within two years, the government of Singapore would revoke his citizenship. But father did not care. All he knew was that he wanted to study with Pyotr Gusiev and become a great dancer.

And so he went. At the Beijing Dance Academy father excelled, graduating at the top of his class. He was offered a place in the Central Ballet of China (now known as the National Ballet of China), one of the country's two major dance companies, and almost immediately he was named a principal dancer. He met another dancer in the company,

My parents before the Cultural Revolution, dancing the leads in The Fountain of Bakchisarai *as partners for the first time.*

Lin Yee, and they fell in love and were married. The eldest of four children, Lin Yee had been picked to join the Beijing Dance Academy at about the age of eleven. Her father had been a bank executive, while her grandfather had been a well-known Chinese painter (almost all of his art was destroyed during the Cultural Revolution). Lin Yee also had a Russian teacher in China, and rose to become a principal dancer at the Central Ballet, until her arthritis forced her to retire early and begin a new career as a teacher.

And so my parents made a good life for themselves in Beijing. The government provided for all the members of the dance company, giving them an apartment, medical care, and everything else they needed. They didn't have material wealth, but at least they had security and could

*Dad and
Mom in
costume for
one of the
Revolutionary
ballets.*

concentrate on their careers. Father became famous as a principal dancer and he loved performing in the great ballets – *Swan Lake, Sleeping Beauty, Giselle, La Fille Mal Gardée*. Even Chairman Mao himself came to see the Central Ballet.

And then came upheaval, not just for the Central Ballet but for the whole country. In 1966 Mao launched the Cultural Revolution, a movement that sought to make China's Communist society more "pure." Professors, engineers, managers, scholars, scientists, and even artists, musicians, and writers had their jobs and sometimes their homes taken way. Older customs and cultures, and any Western influence were also considered harmful and had to be eradicated. Young people, calling themselves the Red Guards, were encouraged to attack their own teachers and to destroy ancient and beautiful monuments, shrines, and statues. Soon the Cultural Revolution grew out of control. Many were falsely accused and countless millions of people suffered. Farming and industry declined and, in the countryside, people starved.

My father feared for himself and Lin Yee. Any Western influence was now considered corrupting – he was from a Westernized country,

Singapore, and had even lived in "decadent" London. He was not the son of a peasant or a worker or a soldier – the heroes of the Revolution – but of an "evil" capitalist businessman. But fortunately, my parents escaped being personally persecuted. Instead, they merely suffered with all the other dancers as the quality of life declined and it became forbidden to perform the great Western ballets.

Mao's wife, Jiang Qing, a former movie actress, took charge of China's culture. She banned the entire repertoire of Western ballet, permitting only new ballets that celebrated the Chinese Revolution. These ballets could not be love stories, as so many of the old Western ballets were, with their beautiful pas de deux that express love and passion between a man and woman. Instead they had to be stories that showed Chinese peasants, workers, and soldiers as heroes willing to sacrifice themselves for the country. Nor could the style of dance be romantic or lyrical; it had to be harsh and bold, showing the strength of the Chinese people. Leotards and tights were too revealing and could no longer be worn.

The best known of these new ballets were *The White Haired Girl* and *The Red Detachment of Women*. As a principal dancer, my father not only performed in them, but played the leading male roles so that his fame as a dancer continued. But after years of perfecting his refined artistry, he found the harsh, folkloric movements demanded by these parts hard to adapt to. Nor could he, the son of a businessman, feel much relationship to the stories they told. For the next years he and my mother had to perform the same parts over and over and over again, not only in theaters but in factories and villages, on makeshift outdoor stages, in freezing weather. Instead of growing as an artist, my father felt himself shriveling inside. His dream of being a real artist of dance seemed to be over.

And then I was born.

✐✐

CHAPTER 3

BIG RED

O n the night that my mother went into the hospital with labor
pains, my father was performing at the company's theater in
Beijing. After the curtain went down he jumped onto his bicycle and
rode as fast as he could towards the hospital. On the way he looked up
and saw a full moon, huge and glowing red. On the morning of the first
of February I was born. My parents named me Chan Hon – *Hon* is the
color red, and *Chan* means "to rise." One of the first stories I can remember being told is how I got my name. "I'd never seen the moon shine so
brightly as on the night that you were born," my father told me.

Beijing is one of the largest cities in the world, but the world of my
early childhood was very small. The apartment we lived in was part of
a complex of several buildings with a cement wall around it. Everyone
who lived there was either a dancer or affiliated with the ballet company in some way – musicians, costume makers, production people. Less
than a block away was the ballet company's rehearsal studios. Although
our second-floor apartment had two bedrooms, there was a housing
shortage in Beijing and another couple occupied one of them. We

*The secret is
in the landing;
as Kitri in
Don Quixote.*

shared the bathroom, and our family had the larger bedroom with a little balcony. Although Chinese people didn't keep pets, my father, who had an unusual love of animals, used to feed the pigeons there. My parents slept in a double bed and I had a cot. I remember drowsing off to sleep while one of my parents would be reading by lamplight on the other side of the room.

That complex was my world. In the common yard all the kids would play with elastic skip ropes, making up elaborate combinations of movements. We played pick-up sticks with old popsicle sticks, tossing them on the ground and trying to pick them up one at a time without disturbing any of the others. My mother didn't like me to collect the sticks — she thought they were dirty and might carry dangerous germs like tuberculosis — and I remember that once an older girl gave me some of her sticks, which she had washed, because I didn't have any. I put all of them in a cardboard cigarette box (at that time, all the men in China smoked cigarettes) and carried them happily home. But when I got up again from my nap I discovered that my mother had thrown them away. I was so mad and made such a fuss and felt so mistreated that finally my mother went out and, even though we had no extra money for such things, bought me a set of the packaged sticks sold in stores. But they weren't the same — nobody used packaged sticks. How unjust the world could be sometimes!

When I was about four and not yet in school, my Mother taught me how to write in calligraphy my nickname, Da Hong, which means "Big Red." I wasn't called big because I was big — in fact, I was a small child — but because I was the first born. One day our neighbor was painting his door frame in bright purple, and I borrowed one of the smaller brushes and painted my name on the white wall beside our own door. After all, without my name by the door how would any of the other kids find me? But my parents were horrified. Not only did my name on the wall violate our privacy, but it brought attention to us, when in China the important thing was to show

My name, in Chinese characters.

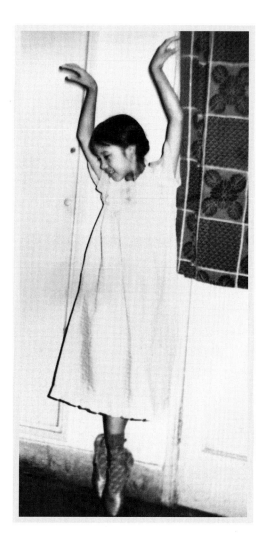

Imitating
a photo of
Aunt Soo Nee
– in my nightie,
my wool socks,
and my mother's
pointe shoes.

that you were just like everybody else. And because paint, like so many things, was hard to come by, they had to wait a number of weeks before finding some white paint to cover over my purple name.

I suppose that I had a little stubborn streak as a child, with my own definite ideas. I would get indignant if my parents couldn't convince me that what I wanted to do was wrong. But most of the time I was happy in our little world, playing with the other kids, looking for my mother or father in one of the rehearsal halls. Being an only child, I was always looking to make friends. I wanted people to like me and I wanted to fit in – traits that have never left me. But on my own, I could keep myself busy too. Sometimes when my parents were in rehearsal or teaching, I'd stay in the apartment and open my mother's shoe box. I'd slip on her pointe shoes and dance around the apartment, holding myself up and imitating the ballet dancers. Actually, wearing pointe shoes when you are too young can be damaging to the feet, and I sometimes got blisters or broken skin on my toes. Was I thinking about becoming a ballerina? Probably I was just having fun pretending, and what was more likely for me to imagine? Dancing was just a part of life; it was what my parents did every day, what they talked about. Sometimes my mother, who began teaching not long after I was born, would bring me with her to the studio. Sometimes I'd get to see a performance. Those Revolutionary ballets might have become dull to my father, but they were exciting to me and I would dance in the aisles of the theater.

As much as the dancing, it was the stories that thrilled me when I was a kid. For that same reason I loved the Chinese musicals that we saw on television. It wasn't until I was about five that televisions became affordable enough for people like us to buy one, and there weren't a lot of programs. But I just adored those musicals, with stories a lot like the Revolutionary ballets. One was about a farmer and his daughter who aided the Revolution by hiding a soldier in the house, deceiving the evil landlord. Somehow I was able to remember the songs afterwards and I would imitate the actors, singing and gesturing in a manner that quite impressed my parents. In fact, it made them think that I might have a future as a singer, and later in Canada I did take some singing lessons. But what I was really responding too, just as I did with the ballets, was the emotional drama of the characters.

Life would have been more idyllic if I could have just stayed in our little apartment, but both my parents worked, and their performance schedules (my father in lead roles, my mother in minor ones because of her arthritis) often kept them too busy to take care of me. And so in my earliest years I often stayed with a nanny who lived just across the street from our apartment, a grandmotherly woman whose children had already grown up. I liked her well enough; what I detested was the daycare that my parents put me into when I was about five. At this daycare, where the kids also slept at night, it was as regimented – or so it felt to me – as if I had suddenly joined the army. I remember saying to one of the caregivers, "I'm not ready to go to sleep. Can you read me a story?" And her reply: "No story. Everybody has to go to bed now." The bungalow room with the row of little beds was very dark, and I was used to falling asleep with a light on (it is a habit I still have). To have a little more comfort, I asked my mother to bring me an extra blanket on one of her weekend visits. The blanket, I knew, would smell of home. I never learned to like the daycare any better and, after a month with my parents in the summer, I screamed all the way there on the first day back. My mother's heart softened and she let me return to the nanny across the street for the rest of the year.

After that came grade one, my first year of school. My parents, who had particular values, made a point of enrolling me in a smaller school with a good reputation rather than the one near our apartment. They had to say that my permanent address was actually my grandmother's in order for me to get in. In that year, I started to learn to write the complex Chinese calligraphy, practicing by trying to make all the strokes and marks of each character inside the lines of a box. Here, as in all the subjects, I had a great eagerness to get good marks and win the approval of my teachers and parents. Of course whenever I did well or wrote a little poem I would be praised by the adults, and I was always hungry for such words. This need carried through to my early years of ballet training when I hoped for a good word from my father, who was my teacher, or from the visiting choreographers and teachers who would come to class. It was as if I couldn't judge myself and always needed someone to confirm for me that I was a worthy person. And in grade one, I liked hearing that I was a good girl and a smart one.

That was why I was so eager to earn my red scarf. Red is the symbol of Communism and in school a red scarf, like a girl-scout badge

My first red scarf — the cotton one. We sent this photo to my dad in Vancouver.

but even more meaningful, said that you were a valuable, worthy person who matched the ideals of the Communist child. And if you didn't get one — well, that implied that you were a poor student, a bad learner, and maybe even not Communist in your way of thinking. Having such a need for approval, I wanted to be among the first group in my class to earn one, and so I tried hard to be nice to the other kids, to succeed in my studies, and to help with cleanup and other chores. As a result I got chosen as one of the first group.

My mother had kept her own red scarf all those years, a beautiful silk one instead of the usual cotton, but my parents were not sure if I ought to wear it. Being a good Communist meant not standing out too much, not making yourself different or special in any way, and my parents feared that the silk scarf would make it look like I was showing off. And so they decided against it and found an old cotton scarf, with a little rip in it. My aunt ironed it smooth and I wore that one instead. Only later did my mother decide it would be all right for me to wear the silk scarf.

Having met my paternal grandmother for the first time just days before this photo was taken, I was on my best behavior for our outing to the Great Wall.

This desire of mine to be a good girl who won praise was balanced by my stubborn streak and a strong personal sense of right and wrong. This side of me came out on the eve of my father's retirement from dancing. The professional life of a dancer is not long, and my father was by then past thirty-five and had a back problem. Like my mother, he had started to teach, and when I was five or six he decided it was time to give up dancing altogether. Perhaps he was also just tired of the limited roles he was allowed to dance, or he was already considering leaving China and thought that the government would not let him dance once he requested permission for us to emigrate. For his last show he was to play the male lead in *The White Haired Girl*, the role of the neighbor who becomes a soldier and saves the white-haired girl and her family.

We were preparing to go to the theater when my maternal grandmother accused me of doing something. I cannot now remember what she claimed I did, but I can relive perfectly the pained outrage I felt on being falsely accused. My grandmother would not back down and admit that she might be wrong, and so I went into a fit of hysterical crying, as if that might prove my innocence. As a result we were late for the performance, missing the first act in which my father had his most spectacular dancing. We saw only the second act, and that from high up in the balcony, because my mother was always nervous watching my father and didn't like to sit too close. And so I can remember nothing of my father's performance that night, only the burning sensation of having been wronged, and to this day I am sorry that I have no recollection of my father's last dance.

✲

I could not have imagined that I would one day leave this little world behind; I could hardly imagine that there even was another world beyond this one. During the Cultural Revolution people in China were rarely allowed to visit other countries, and even within China it was necessary to have special permission to travel. Only once did we get to see some of the country, when I was seven and my father's mother came to visit us from Canada. We all went together on a tour of four Chinese cities.

I didn't know it at the time, but it was on that tour that my grandmother urged my father to try to bring us all to Canada, where there would be so many more opportunities and a greater promise of a good life for me. My father's other relatives also ended up urging him to try to emigrate, even though it was a risk even to tell the Chinese government that you wanted to leave. Asking permission to leave was considered a criticism of the country, and although the Cultural Revolution was coming to an end — even the Chinese government would eventually admit that it was a catastrophe — those who dared to criticize the country still risked being punished. My father spent many tormented nights agonizing over what to do. Could we start a new life from nothing? Would he remember the English he had learned so long ago in London, and would my mother and I be happy? How would he earn a living? He was thirty-seven and his own dancing career had come to an end, but he had found a new calling as a teacher. To leave behind the world of the Central Ballet and all their dancer friends was almost impossible to imagine. And yet what was there really for us in China? The country had been at a virtual standstill for years. He did not know what I might do when I grew up, but how many choices would I even have in China? If we were in Canada, our family could make a new start, and he could take care of his aging mother in Vancouver. *Yes, we must leave,* Father decided.

After my grandmother's visit, my parents told me that there was a possibility of us moving to Canada, but that I should not mention it to anyone. They themselves did not mention it again for at least six months, and so I never thought about it. Only when my father received his permission papers to leave China did they speak to me about it again. The government had withheld permission for my mother and me, trying to make the decision more difficult for my parents. But they decided that if my father went first, the government would relent and allow us out as well. And so in one month's time my father would leave us for Vancouver, Canada. He would have a chance to establish himself and, with luck, we would eventually receive our own permission papers and be able to join him. How long would that be? My parents didn't know.

The prospect of traveling to another place was exciting to me, and yet I hardly knew what to think. I simply had no mental image of what Canada was going to be like and how it might be different from China. We saw no Western television, movies, or books of any kind. Because wanting to leave the country was almost considered being a traitor, my mother didn't even want to point out the new country on a map. My father was heading off into unknown territory and one day – or so we hoped – we would follow him.

CHAPTER 4

SLOW BIRD

My mother and I lived in Beijing without my father for a year. It was unusual for a child not to have both parents around, and even stranger that one of them had gone abroad. I was careful not to speak about my father or of our hope of joining him when talking to the other kids.

Meanwhile, we knew that my father was struggling to earn a living and establish himself in this mysterious city called Vancouver. While he considered trying to return to a career in dance, none of the three major Canadian dance companies — the Royal Winnipeg Ballet, the National Ballet of Canada, and Les Grands Ballets Canadiens — was in Vancouver. In truth, when it came to the arts, Vancouver was more on the level of a town than a big city. But to move somewhere else meant not being near his mother, and he wanted to look after her. Besides, at his age he would not have had many years left to perform. So instead, he made up his mind to try to establish a teaching career. His own experience studying in Singapore, in London, and with the Russian master in China, as well as his dance career with the Central Ballet and his subsequent

In costume for a photo shoot in the park.

study for teaching, gave him a background virtually unmatched by anyone in Vancouver.

He was fortunate to earn the position of ballet master to the Anna Wyman Dance Company. It was a small company of less than a dozen dancers who performed in contemporary works rather than ballets, but my father led them in morning classes to improve their technique. That alone wasn't enough work for him to support himself, never mind a wife and child, and so he began to teach classes at already-established dance studios — not to professionals, but to housewives looking to keep fit, as well as kids. This hard work was less than artistically satisfying for someone used to dancing and teaching at the highest levels. After a while he had enough loyal students to begin conducting his own classes in a basement studio.

For twenty years my father had needed to worry only about dance; the government had taken care of everything else. Now he had to pay his studio rent, find and keep new students, not to mention feeding and clothing himself and a hundred other things (including worrying about us) that kept him constantly exhausted and under stress. An artist by temperament, he suddenly had to learn how to be an entrepreneur. Being a dancer gave my father an unusual background for an immigrant, but he had all the same immigrant's cares weighing heavily on his shoulders. He had to struggle to communicate, having discovered that his English was much poorer than he had hoped. He had to learn all the little things — how to take a bus or shop for food — that people raised in Canada took for granted. And although he was lucky to have his sister Soo Nee and her family in Vancouver to stay with, he still had to deal with feelings of isolation and loneliness. The West was more free, but it could also be a much harder place to survive. Neglecting to take care of himself, he lost weight and his hair grew past his ears.

In the spring of 1977, my mother told me that we had finally gotten our papers to leave China. We still needed our airline tickets, but we could expect to depart in a month's time. How happy I was! The thought that I would soon see my father made every other aspect of leaving unimportant. All I could imagine was seeing him again. I didn't think about leaving the other kids behind or what I would have to learn in my new life. My grandmother said to me, "You will have to learn English. You should work hard so as to do well in school and not get left behind." But I didn't pay much attention.

It is always harder to learn a language as an adult and to adapt to a new life, so my mother was, if anything, going to face even greater hardships and challenges than I would. But she didn't have time to think about that. She ran about the city getting the necessary stamps and signatures, and doing everything else needed to prepare for our departure. A week before we were set to leave she decided to take us both to get our hair done so that we would look nice when we saw my father for the first time. I had never had anything but a basic cut with bangs, and I felt tremendously excited. And so one afternoon the two of us went to the beauty parlor and had our hair permed. A huge helmet-like machine was placed over my head; it felt as if my hair was being electrocuted. Afterwards, my mother was devastated; our heads had been turned into huge curly balls, Afro styles that just didn't suit us. I didn't really mind, but back home my mother kept wetting our curls to try to keep them down.

Whether we looked silly or not, it was time for us to leave. My grandmother, who was a very strong woman, became depressed with the thought that she was losing her daughter to a faraway country and started to cry, a sight I had never witnessed before. It was then I realized what an enormous event this was for our entire family. I myself didn't make any formal good-byes to the other kids in the apartment complex. All I could think was that I was going to be with my father again, so how could I possibly miss anything?

✴

Our plane flew from Beijing to Hong Kong, where we stayed for five days with a distant cousin of my father's. While I happily played with my two girl cousins, my mother went out shopping for clothes and a set of dishes that would be shipped over to Canada. Once we got there, she saw the hardship that my father had endured to save up the money for our tickets and decided that she shouldn't have spent anything at all.

We also went to a salon in Hong Kong where our hair was made to look somewhat better. And then came the long plane ride to Canada, during which I slept a good deal. My mother woke me when the meal came, and I saw a strange vegetable that we had never eaten in China. It looked like green cauliflower to us, and only later did I learn that it was called broccoli. On the side was a little package of soy sauce that was so small and pretty I wanted to save it. This was the beginning of so many encounters with newness for me. For the moment we could marvel at these things without yet having to confront the more difficult realities of the new life that lay ahead of us.

My father was fearful that we might get lost at the airport in Vancouver since neither of us spoke any English, so he had us met at the gate by one of his students who worked for an airline. She guided us through the terminal to an empty waiting area and there, sitting in a chair, was my father. The image I had carried of him all these months was not matched by the man I saw. This man was too thin. His hair was ragged. And at the same time I knew right away that I could put my arms around him and he was the same father I had always known.

The meeting between my parents was more restrained, but in China kisses and even hugs in public were rare. My aunt and uncle were waiting in the car to drive us to their house. It was in their basement at 58th and Oak Street in south Vancouver that we would live for the next year. And over the next days we stayed pretty much around the house, getting used to my father's teaching schedule; he was always running off to one dance studio or another. I was sorry that my cousins were teenage boys who had little interest in playing or even talking to me, but I was so glad for our family to be all together again that I could feel no disappointment. Of course there were adjustments we had to make to learn to live in our relatives' house, sharing the upstairs kitchen. And again so many things were new. In Beijing we did not have a refrigerator, and clothes had all been washed by hand and hung to dry instead of in a washing machine and dryer.

Back in China I had been given a couple of simple English books and a set of alphabet cards. But really I knew no English at all, and in the fall I was expected to enter school with the other kids. So my father arranged for me to go to summer school, where kids went for extra help. It was far from the house and each morning my father had to take me on the bus. I wish this first experience had been a good one, but instead it was extremely painful because I simply couldn't talk to the other kids. While there were some other minorities, I was the only Chinese child, and I was shut out of the play. Recess was a nightmare. I would want to join some kids on the swings or at the teeter-totter or playing ball, but when I approached they would scream names at me.

"Chink! Retard!"

I didn't have to understand the meaning of the words to know that they were insulting me, and finally I confessed to my father about my humiliation. He took it as a personal blow that I should be treated this way but, as he still felt unfamiliar with Canadian ways, he decided to consult a friend of his who was a musician with the Vancouver Symphony. The friend helped my father write a letter to the teacher, telling her how left out I felt and how hurt I was by the name calling. The next school day I gave the letter to the teacher and, after she read it, she gave me such a warm and kind look that I felt reassured for the first time. Then she went outside to speak to the other kids. After that they became much nicer to me. I still got the occasional dirty look or comment about "contaminating" the playground, but most of the kids made an effort to be friends and some of them even invited me to join their games. I went home much happier that day and my father, eagerly waiting to know what happened, was glad that he had found a way to help me.

The assumption by other kids that I was stupid because my language skills were behind was something that continued to dog me for at least three years, until my English caught up. My teenage cousins were

In rehearsal, I never mind doing steps over and over in order to get them right.

honor-roll students and my cousins in Singapore were also always getting achievement awards or scholarships, bringing honor to the family. But because I was behind, I felt myself to be inadequate. And seeing how I had been treated by the other kids, I thought that unless I could speak well and excel in school I would always be treated as an outsider. Some people become resentful and rebellious when treated badly, but I remembered an old saying that my grandmother told me back in China. "Slow birds fly earlier," she had said. My grandmother was telling me that I might seem behind the other kids when I got to Canada, but if I got an earlier start each day and put in more time and effort, I would eventually catch up. Remembering her words, I had an urge to prove myself. I would show them just how smart and accomplished I could be.

We lived in my aunt and uncle's basement for a year and a half before my parents felt financially confident enough to rent our own place, the upper floor of a house in a nice neighborhood. We all considered this a real step forward in our new life. By now my mother was also teaching in the basement studio; my parents had given their own classes the rather grand name of the Goh Ballet Academy.

Moving to a new neighborhood meant switching to a new school, another hardship to endure. Not only was my English still weak, and my knowledge of Canadian ways still insecure, but I had to try to fit into a school where most of the kids had known one another since kindergarten. In order for me to be with my age group, the school decided to let me skip grade four, which made it even harder to catch up to the other kids in reading and writing. And because I was the only Chinese person in class, the kids considered me different. It didn't help matters that I was no good in gym, a place where a kid could earn popularity by hitting a ball or running fast. Only in grade six did I start to do a lot better on my written work and get higher grades, but the teacher and I did not get along and he made life tough for me. Still, with my English reaching the level of the other kids, who had known me long enough to become my friends, and my grades rapidly improving, I began to feel better about myself.

Coming from an artistic family, it was only natural that my parents would want me to take some classes outside of school. But they did not imagine me a dancer, or encourage me in any way to think seriously about ballet. No, it was musical talent that they saw in me and tried to encourage, first with piano lessons in China and then with singing lessons in Vancouver – they remembered those Chinese musicals I loved to imitate – before going back to the piano. In fact, it was for playing the piano that I seemed to have a natural ability, and my parents encouraged me to work hard. My piano teachers and also my uncle, who was a professor of music at the University of British Columbia, all thought

I had a real chance of becoming a concert pianist. I had big hands that, as I grew older, could reach more than an octave, and I could "articulate" my fingers very, very quickly. But I did not enjoy practicing piano – it was such a solitary pursuit, requiring hour after lonely hour at the keyboard.

In contrast to my natural abilities at the piano, as a dancer it was my weaknesses that were most obvious. I took my first ballet class at the age of nine, not with my mother or father, who didn't have proper children's classes going yet, but with my Aunt Soo Nee. Soo Nee was the older sister who had gone to the Royal Ballet in London before my father, and she taught at a well-established academy in the city. Most of the other kids had started classes when they were only five years old, and when I joined them they were already in grade two for dance. But catching up here wasn't so difficult, as a nine-year-old quickly learns to imitate. Besides, I had watched dance all my life. Just like an adult class, we started at the barre – a long rail against the wall for holding on to – while doing various exercises in our leotards and soft shoes. After that we moved away from the walls to do center work. It was mostly a matter of trying to get the basic body positions right, but my Aunt Soo Nee was an inspiring teacher and she made us all feel like real ballerinas. At the barre we practiced doing the plié, bending at the knee in the turnout position – feet pointing outward – a fundamental exercise because it begins and ends almost every step in choreography. And just doing a plié, it was clear that I lacked some natural qualities for dance. My turnout was not good, and the plié movement itself came out small rather than full because of the short, tight tendons in my legs. Nor was I very coordinated at that age, so I had trouble controlling my long arms. When my father saw me in class, he saw these drawbacks and concluded that, despite some good qualities – such as a natural grace despite my child's clumsiness – I did not have the makings of a dancer.

I practiced piano every day, as I was told to – but only because I was told to.

Coming from a dance family, I was aware of these faults almost from the start. But they didn't much matter to me. I was taking dance only once a week, hardly seriously, and it was enough that I enjoyed the class and felt inspired for the hour by Aunt Soo Nee. And so I took classes for two years with my aunt, by which time my mother had started her own classes for kids in the basement studio and I began to take some of hers as well. I passed my dance exams for grades two and three with "commended" and then, at the age of eleven, continued on with my mother and father, taking two classes a week after school and one on Saturday.

But it was still just for fun. Instead of having to practice for hours alone at the piano, I got to hang out with other girls my age. My English had caught up, and at school I had moved to the top of my class. My parents were busy from morning to night, taking care of me while running the Goh Ballet Academy. My grandmother, who I called Lau Lau (the name for maternal grandmother in northern China), had come to Vancouver to help look after me. She and I spoke Mandarin so that I wouldn't lose the language. Always valuing the importance of family, she made sure that we all ate dinner together each evening. The small, lonely girl still existed somewhere inside me, but I was happier now.

And then things started to get serious.

CHAPTER 5

IF YOU WANT TO BE A DANCER . . .

S ometimes it helps to cry. Or to do something in order to get noticed, as I was soon to find out.

In our first years in Vancouver my parents built up the curriculum at the Goh Ballet Academy, and every year the kids would advance, giving my father and mother older, more accomplished students to teach. My parents' teaching was based on the main principles of the Vaganova method, as passed to them by their Russian teachers. It wasn't long before their students began winning awards at local ballet competitions. Other parents and teachers noticed not only their fine dance training but also the quality of the choreography — my father's — and even their costumes. My father also formed the Goh Ballet Company, a semi-professional group of adult dancers, to perform in small theaters. Slowly my parents helped to raise the standard of dance instruction in the city, but even in the early years their reputation developed quickly. By 1981, the basement studio had become inadequate and the school moved to the much nicer Acadian Hall building on Main Street, with one large and one smaller studio space on the second floor. Professional dancers

I was determined to match Rex Harrington's strength and support myself as Spring in The Four Seasons.

visiting Vancouver would come and join an open class and, when I was about eleven, Evelyn Hart, star of the Royal Winnipeg Ballet, booked a few private lessons with my father. All the young girls – including me – were just mesmerized by this renowned dancer coming to our little studio. In time, my father was invited to visit the Royal Winnipeg Ballet as a guest teacher, and was also asked to guest teach at York University, the Banff School of Fine Arts, and schools in other countries.

As for me, I was getting more hooked on dance from watching the performances of the Goh Ballet Company, and especially seeing the pas de deux work between the male and female dancers. How thrilling it must be, I thought, to be lifted high and do so many turns with a partner. But the main reason was that I was part of a group of girls, all of us about twelve years old, who wanted to take classes more often. And so I quit the piano in order to dance four times a week in longer classes. Dance became our major interest and even passion. Both my parents taught us, my mother instructing us in pointe work (which began at about age eleven), the fundamental positions, and accuracy of technique, while my father concentrated on artistic expression and style. Like most girls, I was glad to begin pointe – my image of a real ballet dancer was always up on her toes. Despite my other physical shortcomings, I had strong ankles and arches that weren't overly pronounced, as well as the courage it takes to get up on pointe. Being on pointe seemed to me almost natural.

From both my parents, I learned everything I could. In time, my parents designated us as the Professional School Program to differentiate us from the kids who took dance more casually, coming just once or twice a week. As in all ballet classes, we began with barre work and then moved on to center work, afterwards working on a little choreographed piece based on the ballet repertoire. We all loved practicing these little dances, usually on Saturday when we would stay for an extra hour. One day Father decided to choreograph a group dance for us using the music of the Waltz of the Flowers from *The Nutcracker*. It was tremendous fun for us and made us feel like real dancers, and my father took us to one of the local festivals where we performed it for the judges.

From the earliest age, dancers must get used to being watched and judged. We practice in front of mirrors, which makes us critical of ourselves. We listen to our teachers give us constant corrections – showing us how this foot or that arm is not placed properly. We compete in competitions and perform for audiences of our families and friends. Even for a young dancer, being constantly judged becomes second nature. But at our first festival we were all having fun, and so we were surprised and thrilled when the announcement came that we had won the first-prize trophy.

And so I began to live, breathe, and dream ballet. Even when I wasn't taking classes, I would be hanging about the studio with the other kids in our new Professional division. We would even join classes below our level just to get extra practice. And we had started to learn about the real world of professional ballet. We knew the names of all the stars of the American Ballet Theatre and the New York City Ballet, whose performances would sometimes be shown on American public television – Gelsey Kirkland, Cynthia Harvey, Peter Martins. We also knew about the great Russian dancers who had defected to the West – Rudolf Nureyev, Natalia Makarova, and Mikhail Baryshnikov. We knew about the famous choreographer George Balanchine, and that his favorite ballerina at the New York City Ballet was Suzanne Farrell. We would read *Dance Magazine* and find out which dancer was leaving her company because she didn't get along with the director. Unfortunately, we knew much less about the Canadian dance companies, mostly because their performances were rarely shown on television. Sometimes we would hear of Karen Kain and Frank Augustyn at the National Ballet of Canada, and Evelyn Hart at the Royal Winnipeg Ballet, but that was all.

But even while the intensity of my own interest was increasing, something was deeply upsetting me. My teachers – who also happened to be my parents – did not seem to notice how hard I was working. I

*At age 13,
in costume for
a solo at a
local festival
competition.*

needed outside praise in order to believe in my own self worth, and my
father especially was not providing them. Not only did he pay me no
special attention, but he seemed to concern himself with me *less* than he
did with the other kids. He praised them more often, scrutinized their
movements more closely, corrected them more frequently. Me, he took
for granted. Being someone with strong feelings about fair treatment, it
was only natural that my boiling emotions would finally erupt.

I was thirteen years old when, one day after class, we came back
home. My parents began talking about the students in my Professional
class – who was the most technically accomplished, who the most
expressive, who had the greatest chance to make it as a dancer. And
suddenly I could not stop myself from speaking. "You know," I said to
my father, tears already beginning to well in my eyes, "I was in all of
those classes today too. You never even notice. I don't know what the
other girls have got that I don't. I try just as hard. How come you never
correct me or praise me like you do the others?"

By this time I was really crying. My father did not know how to respond and remained silent. It was my mother who had to calm me down. "Of course he would have noticed," she said. "Your dad has enough love to go around for everyone. It's not that he doesn't notice you. But he feels obligated to these other people because of their financial commitment to the school. He thought of you as his daughter and didn't know that you were actually that focused."

As for my father, I didn't realize that his own emotions had choked all the words in his throat. He had not meant to upset his only beloved daughter. How could he not have noticed how serious I was? In truth, he had watched me and had seen some of my shortcomings – my turnout, my flexibility. He had observed that I could not raise my leg as high as my mother had been able to in her dancing years, all the way to her nose. But now he spoke. "All right," he said "If you really want to be a dancer then I will work with you. I will watch you and correct you. Everything I can, I will do. From now on, I will take care of you."

My father was true to his word. Even now, after training with many world-class dance teachers and guest performing under so many artistic directors at different companies, I have not found a teacher quite as nurturing as he was. And not just for me, but for all his students. In fact, it always seemed to me that my parents treated each one of their students as their own child, whose future was important to them. And the key to their approach was encouragement. Yes, Father could be strict, but he believed that encouragement and stimulation would get better results. So he would patiently demonstrate a step or combination over and over, and his combinations – standard steps put together – were always rhythmical and interesting. They would help to train a young dancer's mind as well as her body.

I was glad to get equal attention from my father, and to be considered a serious student at last. As for my father, he really did begin to consider whether I might have the talent for a career. Perhaps it was hard to judge his own child and what he needed was the opinion of someone else; if so, he soon got it, although unbeknownst to me. My father read in the Vancouver newspaper that the legendary Anton Dolin was in town. A dancer for the great Diaghilev in the 1920s, Dolin had later become founder and artistic director of London's Festival Ballet. Dolin had wanted my father to join his company when he was a teenager studying in London, but Father had gone to China to study with the Russians instead. Now my father rushed to the hotel where Dolin was staying and found his old mentor with white hair and using a cane for support. The two had an emotional reunion, Dolin asking my father what had happened to him, and my father recounting his decades in China. Then my father, always looking for opportunities for his students, asked Dolin if he would come and teach a class at the academy.

Dolin came to class, but he was old and frail, and asked my father to teach the class while he watched. Or perhaps he just wanted to see how good a teacher my father was. And so he sat and observed our Professional class, and we girls were excited to have this great ballet figure in the studio with us. After class, Dolin called my father aside. He pointed to one of the students. "That one," he said. "She has it. Yes, she is going to be a beautiful dancer."

My father tried to see which girl he was pointing at. Dolin seemed to be pointing at me, but my father thought he must be mistaken – there were girls in class who were better. To make sure, he called me over. I did not know what they had been speaking about, so when my father said, "You are talking about her?" I didn't understand what he meant.

"Yes," said Anton Dolin.

"She is my daughter," said my father.

"Ah, you see?" His old mentor smiled.

My father sent me back to my friends. He did not tell me then what Anton Dolin had said, worrying that his words would make me too sure of myself. But he took them in.

Practicing: the desire to improve and the pursuit of perfection.

My mother, Lin Yee, who had good practical skills, was the principal of the academy, while my father held the title of artistic director of the Goh Ballet Company. And it was the company that provided the immediate inspiration for us young dancers as we watched the adults rehearse and perform. Its members were professionals between full-time jobs, or who had recently retired but still wanted to do some dancing, and good amateurs. They were paid only what little could be spared from the ticket sales. My father, however, had hopes that the company would grow, believing that Vancouver deserved a classical company. But it wasn't because of my father that I was cast in my first leading role, in a ballet called *The Butterfly Lovers*. It was because of a new acquaintance of the academy named Ling Tsui.

A caring, generous, and sophisticated woman, Mrs. Tsui was Chinese but had spent many years living and studying in Paris. She had enrolled her young daughter in the Goh Ballet Academy and took private classes herself, a rarity because of the expense. Later, Mrs. Tsui would become my godmother, and her independence, determination, and cultural refinement would become an example for me. It was she who had acquired for the Goh Ballet the chance to perform *The Butterfly Lovers* at a fundraising event for the Lions Club of Vancouver at the Queen Elizabeth Theatre. And it was she who convinced my father that I be cast as the female lead, telling him that I was clearly the most outstanding young dancer in the school.

So it was because of Mrs. Tsui that my first real public performance had me in a leading role at the age of thirteen. Not only my first performance, but my first pas de deux — and with a male dancer who I had a terrible crush on!

Incredibly captivating, Che Chun was many years my senior and the leading dancer of the Goh Ballet. My father had been one of his teachers back in China, and Che had gone on to become a principal with the Central Ballet, dancing not only the major Revolutionary roles that my father had once performed in, but also in *Swan Lake*, *Don Quixote*, and *Coppélia* once the Chinese government had begun to allow them again. Wanting to broaden his horizons, he had come to Canada the year after my mother and I had, eventually becoming vice-principal of the Goh Academy, where he taught while dancing in the company. He even lived in our house for a time. I had known him since I was a little girl, but now I had started becoming interested in boys, and Che had a wonderful personality. I didn't socialize much at school and, since I looked up to professional dancers, perhaps it was inevitable that I would develop a crush on him. It wasn't that boys my own age didn't interest me, but none of them was involved in my dance world, where I spent almost all my time.

The Butterfly Lovers is a famous Chinese story, in which two young people, deeply in love but unable to marry, find eternal happiness when their spirits are transformed into butterflies. My father decided to choreograph a duet using a combination of Western ballet movements and traditional Chinese dance, with the woman dancer in soft shoes rather than pointe. Not having done any partnering, this was an enormous and also frightening learning experience for me. During rehearsals, Che would lift me into the air and I would scream, afraid of being dropped. He would tell me to hold myself solidly, and I tried, but he said I felt as wobbly as Jell-o. Each rehearsal was exhausting, since he was the experienced one and all the corrections were on me. Quickly I forgot about my crush; this was about the hard work of dancing and nothing else. I was very fortunate to have such an accomplished dancer as my first partner. We could skip the usual tedious exercises and move right into the choreography, with Che guiding me on every step. Much later, as a professional dancer, I would sometimes be partnered with young, hesitant male dancers who made me feel less than sure that they would catch me on the way down.

The Queen Elizabeth Theatre is very large; it was the house where the major ballet companies played in Vancouver while on tour. Our performance went well and received warm applause, and I felt that I was no longer terrified of being lifted or of giving my trust to a good partner. Che was happy too, and we took our bows and smiled at one another.

At Mrs. Tsui's backyard pool party, Che lifted me to the top of the world.

The gift Che gave me before the show – a swan-shaped mirror – hangs now in my living room, and I especially remember the card that accompanied it, which said, "May this be a grand jeté to a brilliant career."

Grade eight and high school were a relief to me. Having been around adults so much as an only child, I welcomed the more mature atmosphere. And my marks were now putting me on the honor roll, an accomplishment that brought me tremendous satisfaction. I had entered one of the happiest periods of my life, which seemed as if it would continue forever.

Now that I was serious about dance and my parents were behind me, my mother decided we should all go to New York. She had gone once with a former student and was so inspired by the dance atmosphere created by the studios, teachers, and great ballet companies that she thought I would benefit from the experience. And so she took out a loan and the three of us, along with Che and another student, went for almost two weeks. We stayed in the Chinatown apartment of a friend's friend, bunking down in sleeping bags. During the day my parents took me to open classes, sometimes four a day – the first time I had instruction from teachers who were not members of my family. At night we went to see the American Ballet Theatre and the New York City Ballet. We saw Baryshnikov dance in *Don Quixote* one night and then Fernando Bujones dance the same role the next. I saw Suzanne Farrell dance in Balanchine's exquisite *Mozartiana* (I could not have known that one day Suzanne would teach me the same role). And for the second time I met my uncle Choo San.

Choo San, my father's younger brother, was the fourth child in the family to enter dance, after my father and my two aunts. He had been discouraged by his parents – weren't three children in dance enough? – and had gone to university to study biochemistry before starting his career in Europe. Emigrating to the United States, Uncle Choo San had become an acclaimed choreographer and associate director of the Washington Ballet. He had recently created a piece for Baryshnikov at the American Ballet Theatre and so he took us to an ABT rehearsal. We went through the stage door of the famed Metropolitan Opera House and walked into the green room where my uncle introduced us all to the great Baryshnikov himself. I will never forget the dancer's piercing blue eyes as he shook my hand. Then we had the thrilling experience of watching Fernando Bujones and Cynthia Gregory rehearse *Giselle*. Could a fourteen-year-old girl who dreamed of becoming a dancer be more fortunate? I did not think so.

But the trip was also memorable for another and less positive reason. It also revealed that I was susceptible to one of the serious dangers

With Amy Ruth (another dance student) and my charismatic Uncle Choo San inside the Metropolitan Opera House – my very first time in New York.

facing dancers. At about the age of thirteen, I had found myself starting to look heavy. Indeed, my body was going through natural changes due to puberty, and as a result I was growing larger and a little rounder. This was not the image of the perfect, slim dancer that I had in my head from all the professional ballerinas I had seen in performance, on video, and in pictures. And compared to the younger girls at school I was beginning to look – at least in my own eyes – unattractively big. So before the trip to New York I secretly began to diet. Since I knew nothing about nutrition, I simply counted calories, throwing away the lunches my grandmother prepared for me, or slyly spitting out mouthfuls of food into napkins. Instead, I would eat only a single chocolate bar, or a muffin, or some candies – sweets that my body seemed to crave as I grew hungrier.

The diet worked; I did lose pounds, and people began to remark how thin I looked, comments which I took as a compliment whether they were meant that way or not. Despite being busy at the school, my mother noticed and urged me to eat more, but she often wasn't around to make sure. Secretly, I applauded myself for slimming down to a "proper" ballerina look, and even credited my improvements as a dancer to it. But I was unaware that I was starving my body of the fuel and nutrition it needed, not only to dance, but to survive. Only later would I realize that I was at the beginning stage of anorexia nervosa, an eating disorder that afflicts many dancers – as well as other young people – and can result in serious illness, hospitalization, and even death.

In New York, I had been running around from morning to night, taking one class after another. One day during the trip, after I had taken two classes, we were talking about going somewhere to eat. All of a sudden I didn't feel well. I couldn't even speak, but managed only to put my arms around my father just as I fainted.

In a way, my fainting was a blessing, as it alerted my parents to the serious problem I was developing. After that, they were careful to ensure I ate healthy foods in proper amounts, and quickly I regained my strength. I was lucky; some people find it far more difficult or even impossible to break free from anorexic behavior, and later as a professional I would sometimes spot other dancers who were clearly suffering from the illness.

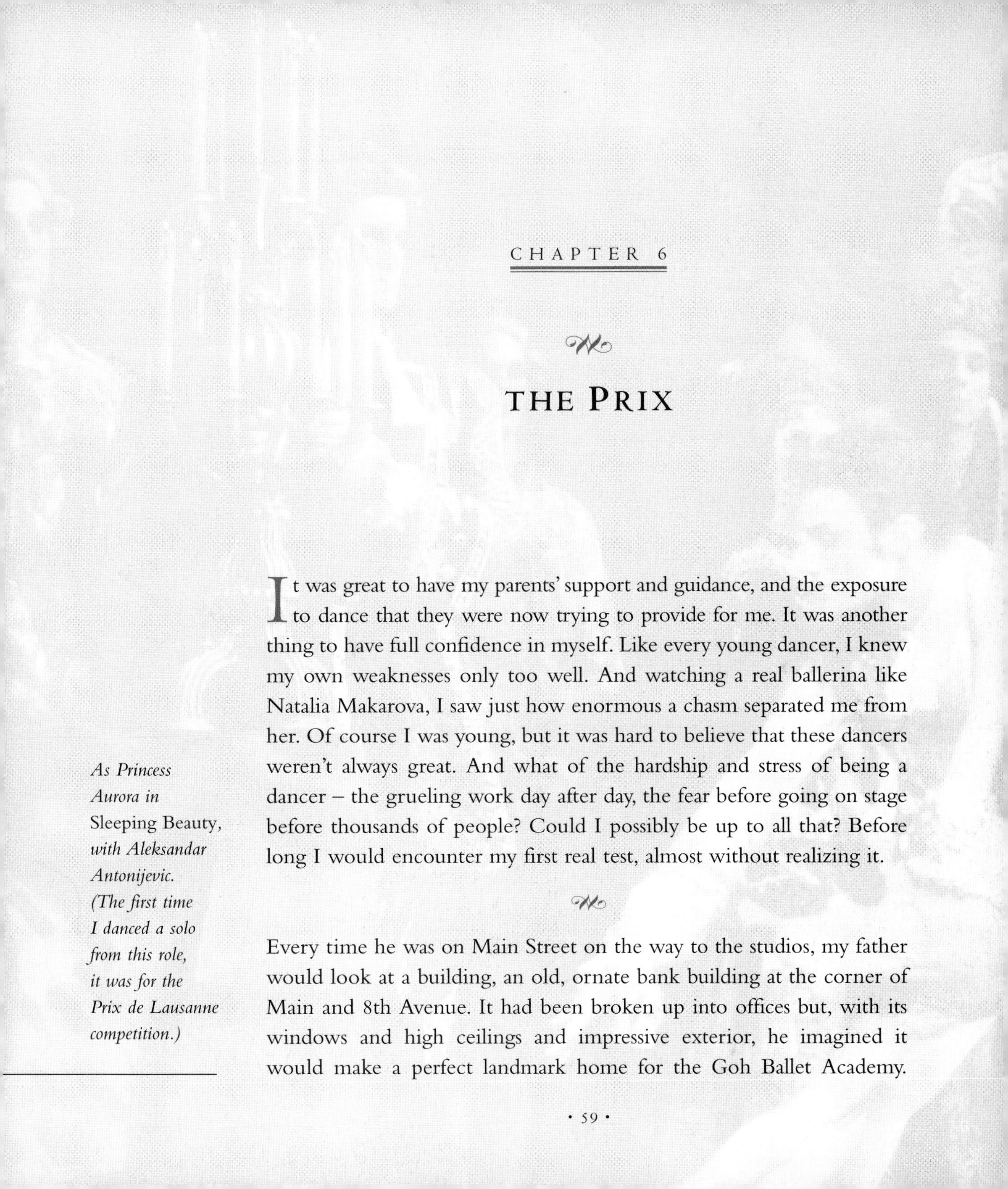

As Princess Aurora in Sleeping Beauty, *with Aleksandar Antonijevic. (The first time I danced a solo from this role, it was for the Prix de Lausanne competition.)*

CHAPTER 6

THE PRIX

It was great to have my parents' support and guidance, and the exposure to dance that they were now trying to provide for me. It was another thing to have full confidence in myself. Like every young dancer, I knew my own weaknesses only too well. And watching a real ballerina like Natalia Makarova, I saw just how enormous a chasm separated me from her. Of course I was young, but it was hard to believe that these dancers weren't always great. And what of the hardship and stress of being a dancer – the grueling work day after day, the fear before going on stage before thousands of people? Could I possibly be up to all that? Before long I would encounter my first real test, almost without realizing it.

Every time he was on Main Street on the way to the studios, my father would look at a building, an old, ornate bank building at the corner of Main and 8th Avenue. It had been broken up into offices but, with its windows and high ceilings and impressive exterior, he imagined it would make a perfect landmark home for the Goh Ballet Academy.

And then one day a For Sale sign appeared in one of the windows. After much consultation and working out of finances, my parents, together with a new partner, Willy Tsao (artistic director of the City Contemporary Dance Company in Hong Kong) managed to buy the building.

It took six months to renovate the interior into four beautiful studios, one with a small spectator's gallery, as well as offices, change rooms, and showers. By 1985 the Academy had moved into its first-class facility, raising Vancouver's level of what a professional school should offer its students in training and facilities. My parents and Che worked tirelessly to run the classes as well as the Goh Ballet Company.

And it was exciting for me to feel a part of it. Wanting more time in the studio, I decided to take grades ten and eleven by correspondence, an option the school board allowed for those with high marks. That way I could do my work in the early morning and evening, and free up the whole day for dancing.

My father saw that I and the other advanced girls in the class could not further our dance technique without male partners. The highlight of so many great ballets are the duets, or pas de deux, between the principal male and female dancers, and partnering takes a great deal of practice and experience. So he began a program to bring male dance students from China, giving them full scholarships to train at the Academy for several weeks at a time and act as our partners. These boys were two or three years older than we were, and already had some partner training, which was a real help. That my father could bring them over showed the marked policy change of the Chinese government from the days when we had left. In his first year in Canada, my father had not been allowed to speak to members of the Shanghai Ballet who had come to Vancouver on tour, an experience that had left him deeply hurt. But now the Chinese were encouraging exchanges with the West.

Dance might have become the center of my dreaming and waking life, but I was certainly not the only girl smitten with dance in the province of British Columbia. There were the other girls in my father's Professional program, as well as the many more at other dance studios,

Age 14, at the Lincoln Center in New York.

and I was by no means recognized as the one who was going to make it. At the local festivals and competitions, if I placed at all it was second more often than first. Although at fifteen I made it to the provincial championship, I didn't win (one of my mother's other students did). But I was never discouraged, for I didn't go into any competition expecting to win. Instead, I was glad for a chance to prepare and then have the experience of being on stage and dancing under pressure. And because I hardly ever won the local prizes, it certainly didn't occur to me to enter a major international competition.

In Vancouver, Aunt Soo Nee was working with a young male dancer from Singapore named Kelly Teo. Kelly had come to Vancouver so that my aunt could help him prepare for the Prix de Lausanne competition in Switzerland. Perhaps the most prestigious competition for young dancers, the purpose of the Prix de Lausanne is to identify the dance stars of the future. The judges look beyond polish and current level of accomplishment to see the talent in a young dancer, the potential for greatness. And it rewards these dancers — there are a dozen or so finalists — by bestowing scholarships to the best ballet schools in North America and Europe.

Not long before, my mother had taken me to England to take some classes at the Royal Academy of Dance and we had watched another important event, the Adeline Genée Competition. I had learned a lot just watching the dancers and so, when Kelly was filling out his application for the Prix, I said to my father, "Maybe we should go and watch. It could be a great experience."

"Yes," my father said, "You're right."

"If you're thinking of going anyway," Kelly said, looking up from the form, "you might as well fill out an application and compete. Why just be a bystander?"

The idea dismayed me. "But I'm not ready," I said. "I don't even have any pieces prepared." I knew from watching Kelly that entrants were not only judged while taking class, but had to perform both a contemporary piece and a classical variation, or solo. And those who made it into the finals needed costumes for their solos, which were performed on stage before an audience.

The application was due in a week, while the competition itself was a mere three weeks away. Most entrants had already spent months in preparation. But that night I thought it over – it occurred to me that during the competition I would turn seventeen – and by morning I knew I wanted to enter. While it seemed unlikely that I would get much past the initial barre section of the competition, what did it matter? The experience would be invaluable.

My parents and I hustled to get in the application, sending it by courier two days before the deadline. After we heard the application was accepted, my father and I had to get to work. I needed to choose a classical variation from the allowed list, and settled on the Aurora variation from Act III of *Sleeping Beauty*. It is the epitome of the style of the great classical choreographer Maurice Petipa, a style that suited me well. Part of the wedding pas de deux, the variation requires very neat footwork, classically precise arm gestures, and a sharp musicality. The dancer must project the elegance of a true princess claiming her throne. More practically, the variation wasn't as technically demanding as some of the others and, considering how little time I had to get ready, it seemed a sensible choice.

In the evenings I watched a video of Natalia Makarova dancing the variation with the American Ballet Theatre and learned it step by step. It had been too many years — before the Cultural Revolution, in fact — since my father had been in a production of *Sleeping Beauty* for him to remember accurately, and I wanted to be exact. And since Makarova was one of my idols, it was only natural that I would want to mimic her expressiveness. So at night I would watch the video, and during the day I would rehearse with my father as coach. I liked working hard in spite of knowing that I probably would be eliminated before getting a chance to dance it. Meanwhile, a costume had to be made. My mother called up a woman who sometimes worked for the Goh Ballet Company, and although she hadn't made very many tutus (they're quite difficult to make) she was eager. It turned out very pretty, and all we needed to do was buy a tiara from the local dance shop.

There was also the problem of the modern solo I was expected to dance. I didn't have anything modern in my repertoire, and in fact had done almost no modern training. It had to be only a minute and forty-five seconds long, which meant that we would have to come up with something ourselves. When my classical variation was coming along, my father and I felt able to look up long enough to consider the question. We decided to ask Che, my first partner and the school vice-principal, to choreograph a piece for me.

By then Che had made the transition from dancer to teacher and choreographer, devising dances for the Goh Ballet Company. The two of us had also started to go out as friends. We went to movies or to a restaurant for a meal after rehearsals. I found him very attractive and his personality fascinating, while his opinions always shed light on issues I felt unclear about. Yet at the same time, I felt I was his equal. As I grew into a young woman, my crush on him was deepening into something more, and I hoped that he was beginning to think of me the same way. But in the studio, we were collaborators only, and after two and a half

Backstage at the semi-finals of the Prix de Lausanne, with students from the Royal Ballet School, Dame Merle Park, and Darcey Bussell (far right).

hours of hard work we came up with the solo. We rehearsed it only twice – the last time the day before the flight – and made a few small refinements. And then, ready or not, it was time to go to Lausanne.

January. Time of colds and fevers. The extra hours I had put in must have worn down my resistance, because when Kelly, my father, and I boarded that airplane I had a blooming cold. The change in altitude made my sinuses pound in my head. Many hours later we were in Geneva and taking a train to Lausanne, with me carrying a big, round tutu bag so the costume wouldn't get crushed. Finally we checked into our hotel and I collapsed for the night.

In the next days I met some of the other competitors; a beautiful American girl named Julie Kent with the perfect made-for-ballet look (she would become a principal dancer with the American Ballet Theatre); an English girl named Darcey Bussell (she would become a principal with the Royal Ballet); as well as dancers from Japan and Europe. In all there were more than a hundred competitors, more than two-thirds of them girls and the rest boys. We had two days to get used to the time change and to rehearse, and then the competition began before the panel of twelve judges. In the bus from the hotel to the theater the other girls stared at me as I furiously blew my nose so that I could breathe a little better. But strangely, the cold didn't affect my mood, most likely because I had no great expectations.

The eighty or so girls were each given a number. During the first round we did exercises at the barre led by an instructor while the judges looked on. Every so often we would move further down the barre so that the judges could get a good look at each of us. Darcey Bussell and I were beside each other, while Julie Kent was about ten numbers behind us, and the three of us went through the competition together. The judges eliminated only a few girls at the barre, after which we went on to center work. Here more entrants were eliminated, and we went on to a little variation exercise on pointe. I survived this round too, and the competition was suspended until the next day.

Unfortunately Kelly, who had been the reason we came, was eliminated from the men's group on the first day. Disappointed but resigned, he made himself content with joining my father as a spectator and encouraging me on. The time arrived for the classical variation, after which thirty or so entrants would be chosen for the semi-finals. We were given the afternoon to rehearse. I practiced the sequence of steps in a circle, called the *manège,* that came towards the end of the solo. This sequence always tired me out anyway, but on the "raked" stage of the theater, I would have to dance them *up* the slope of the stage, which felt like climbing a mountain. Watching the other girls, I was impressed by how technically efficient and strong the Japanese dancers were. "Oh my gosh," I would blurt, "I can't believe that girl is doing so many turns." Or "Look how high she's jumping." But my father always had something to say that would boost my own confidence. "Nobody can shine like you," he told me. "You've got a distinct style. And your musicality stands out." He made me feel special and showed how much he believed in me. We were both happy that I hadn't yet been eliminated; my father felt that coming all the way to Switzerland had already been more than worthwhile. It was an exciting and emotional experience for him, seeing his daughter hold her own against the best young dancers.

The day of the classical variations, February 1, was my seventeenth birthday. Each girl danced in turn and in the evening we gathered to hear the thirty semi-finalists announced, beginning with the lowest number and moving upwards. Some girls who I thought had danced really well were eliminated and I thought, "Ah well, I can tell my number's not going to be called." But then my number was announced and my father and I hugged in amazement.

The next day the finalists would be chosen. All the finalists were prize winners, but they would compete one last time in the closing performance, after which the various scholarships would be given out. I danced the classical variation again as well as the contemporary piece that Che had choreographed, the piece that I'd had no time to rehearse since arriving and only went over the night before. It was a very long day. In the late evening everyone gathered in the hotel meeting room to await the results. It was past midnight when the ten female finalists were announced. The numbers were called out; my own was not among them.

I had known the unlikelihood of my making it as a finalist, but still I had held onto a glimmer of hope and could not help shedding a few tears. My father comforted me, saying, "You did really well, Chan, and I'm proud of how far you've gotten. We didn't really even prepare properly. You did exceptionally well." So I made myself satisfied with reaching the semi-finals. I was so tired and so relieved that the competition was over that, when we went back to our room, I fell into a deep sleep that lasted all night and well into the next day.

My father, however, could not sleep. He had watched all the dancers, and to his highly discerning eye his daughter deserved to be a finalist. What flaws had the judges seen that he had missed? In the morning he went down to breakfast and came back up to find me still sleeping. Not until one in the afternoon did I wake up. I was famished, but the hotel had stopped serving for the afternoon, so my father took me to the nearby McDonald's. My father anxiously watched me eat. He wanted to get to the theater because the judges were holding a kind of open conference; the dancers who had been eliminated could seek advice, and my father wanted to hear why I hadn't made it to the finals.

We arrived while the judges were still there, sitting in pairs so that the dancers could approach them. My father and I approached the nearest two, one of whom was Suki Schorer from the School of American Ballet. Suki Schorer took one look at me and said, "Why are you here? You should be resting up for the show tonight."

My father said, "But her number wasn't called. She's not a finalist."

"Yes," I agreed. "I didn't hear my number either."

"No, I'm definitely sure you're supposed to be a finalist," Suki Schorer asserted. The male judge next to her was not so sure, but Suki was adamant. "We've got to find out what's going on," she said. And the next thing we knew, Suki was marching us to the office where the heads of both the jury and the competition were.

"I'm sure this girl is supposed to be in the finals tonight," Suki told them. The head of the jury listened and then explained why I had been left out. The Prix jury had to choose a certain number of finalists who were studying at government-funded institutions and a certain number from private ballet schools. I was studying at the Goh Ballet Academy which, the jury head continued, was an institution, and those slots were filled by others chosen ahead of me.

"But I don't come from an institution," I said. "I come from a private school."

This put the two men into a fluster. Such an error had never happened before. By rights I ought to be a finalist, but there were only ten scholarships to give out. Besides, the final competition began in only a few hours and I had not spent the day preparing. They conferred for some time. Somehow another scholarship would have to be found. Then they gave me a choice: I could receive a finalist certificate but not compete tonight, since I was hardly ready. Or, if I really wanted to, I could choose to compete anyway.

"I want to perform," I said.

❦

I did dance that evening, musing to myself that at last I would get to wear the costume that I'd dragged all the way from Canada. I was awarded a Prix de Lausanne Finalist Diploma and a summer scholarship to any of the famous schools. I chose the Rosella Hightower International Dance Centre, in Cannes, France – Rosella Hightower herself then offered me a full year's scholarship. When we returned to Vancouver, tired but elated, the dance critic Max Wyman interviewed me – my very first interview – for the *Vancouver Province*. The local dance community was flabbergasted. Chan Hon Goh a finalist prizewinner at the Prix de Lausanne? But she doesn't even win the competitions around here!

For me, something important changed after the Prix. Until then I hadn't felt sure of my own talents. Of course my parents thought I was good, but maybe they were prejudiced in my favor. At the Prix I had not only danced well, but had proven to myself that I could perform even when under pressure. I had a new confidence, a belief that I really could go through with this dream of being a dancer. I accepted the summer scholarship, rather than the full year, and spent six weeks in Cannes. Many professional dancers came to take classes at the school as well, including stars of the Paris Opera Ballet and the Maurice Bejart Company. It was a heady experience to suddenly be living in this adult environment, with more freedom than I had ever known. Rosella Hightower, watching my progress, told me that my technique was already proficient and that what I needed to do was "virtuoso work" – by which I think she meant I had to take my dancing to the next level of brilliance and expressiveness.

Che came to Cannes too, staying in his own bed-and-breakfast, and for three weeks before my parents joined us we had this time alone. The previous summer, when I was sixteen, I had said to Che, "You have to tell Dad that we are serious. You need to get his approval so we can be truthful about how serious we are. And if he doesn't approve, I want you to take me away to elope!"

I just couldn't talk to my father myself, but Che was nervous about approaching him too. After all, to anyone else our age difference seemed large. But as an only child, I had always felt adult, and to me Che did not feel so much older. We were so compatible, and the crush I felt

With Rosella Hightower at her studio in Cannes.

because of his princely manners had turned into real love. We could talk about anything and, although being older brought a maturity to his views, I always felt as if we were on the same level. He was generous and calm, qualities that helped me to be a better person.

That summer my father was guest teaching at the Banff School of Fine Arts and Che was dancing there. Che telephoned me and said, "I spoke to your father and he seemed okay about us." My father in turn spoke to my mother, my mother spoke to my grandmother – and in the end we got the approval we wanted. Not to marry yet – I was too young for that – but to see each other with the goal of marrying some time in the future. Cannes was the first time we traveled together without my family nearby. The two of us felt timid in this foreign place, but we had a chance to rely on one another and to explore and deepen our relationship.

I had gone to the Prix, I was training with great teachers, I was in love, and I was seventeen. The world could not seem to hold more promise.

✋

CHAPTER 7

THE WORLD UPSIDE DOWN

I f an unexpected event had not shifted the direction of my career, it is possible that I would have never left Vancouver. In time I might have become a principal dancer with the Goh Ballet, and under my father's artistic direction the company would have grown to become a fully professional company with a larger repertoire, more performance dates, tours in Canada and abroad.

My father was already extending his ambitions for the company. In 1987, when I was seventeen, he and my mother began to organize a Goh Ballet tour of China and southeast Asia, beginning with Beijing and moving on to four other Chinese cities before traveling to Hong Kong, Singapore, Malaysia, and Indonesia. As a member of the company, I was one of about twenty young dancers, most around the age of eighteen or nineteen, and I had a number of leading roles to perform. One was in *The Dream of the Red Chamber*, a kind of Chinese *Romeo and Juliet* that combined Western ballet with traditional dancing, which we had already performed in Vancouver. But I also had a pas de deux from *Sleeping Beauty*, partnering with a young dancer from China, and a role in a piece

As the spirit of Giselle.

called *Ballade* that my choreographer uncle, Choo San Goh, had "made on" me, creating it with the dancers of the Goh Ballet. Although by now I had performed in a few single-evening shows, this would be my first series of performances, when I would be living the life of a working dancer, performing night after night. I would have the chance to become more at ease in front of an audience and to build up the stamina needed to dance a full season.

The logistics of such a tour are enormous, and my parents worked extremely hard until the day we finally left. In retrospect, I know how much stress the planning must have put on them both. The first stop was Beijing, where we arrived after the long flight and were given a half hour to rest in our rooms before meeting in the hotel restaurant for dinner. My father did not appear in the restaurant, and my Aunts Lin Wen and Wen Yee, who still lived in Beijing and had picked us up at the airport, said to me, "Your father has a bad toothache." So we had dinner without him and then I went back to the room to sleep.

In the morning, my father appeared at the rehearsal studio to give us a class and I saw that he was his usual energetic self. I did notice him perspiring a lot, but I knew he was tired from the long trip and the excitement of coming "home." In the afternoon we had a rehearsal at the theater, and left my father at the studio talking with his old friends. But some time later one of the friends appeared at the theater. "Your dad's in the hospital," he said to me. "He's had a heart attack."

I heard the words but I could not comprehend them. My father? The same man who had just given us such a vigorous class this morning? I just could not take it in.

Che hurried with me to the hospital, the sight of which filled me with even more dread. It was such a run-down, dreary place, with dull-eyed patients lined up in the crowded hallways, intravenous lines in their arms. There were so many of them that we could hardly move down the halls, but finally we found my father in a room, hooked up to a monitor and with an IV drip in his arm like the others. His eyes were closed. All I could say was, "Dad." He opened his eyes. I held his hand,

and only at that moment did I understand that my own dear father had really had a heart attack, that he was in a hospital bed and might not be all right. He looked at me and smiled, his breathing shallow, unable to speak. I wanted to ask a nurse or a doctor about his condition, but there wasn't a single one to be seen. I looked at my father and said, "You're going to be okay, you're going to be okay, everything's going to be okay," although I didn't know if I believed it.

Meanwhile, my mother had been found, told of the heart attack, and rushed to the hospital. Fortunately, she knew of a good doctor at the hospital who referred us to a heart specialist. Within an hour the specialist arrived and, after examining my father, suggested that he be transferred to the ward for foreigners, which was newer and had private rooms. We had to help move him to the ward, through a dark connecting tunnel with someone holding a flashlight and others pushing the bed while I held the IV bottle.

Reaching the foreign ward – forbidden territory to the local people – was like entering another world. The rooms were clean, the nurses in bright white uniforms, the hallways carpeted. The heart specialist installed my father in a room and then came out to consult with us. He said that my father's heart attack was severe. "He's still in pain," the doctor said, "so we've given him a morphine shot and he's sleeping. The next twenty-four hours are crucial. We have to hope he doesn't have another attack."

My mother and I were in shock; the possibility of losing my father was just too terrible. In the meantime, somehow the tour had to go on. That very night there was a big reception held for the company by Chinese government officials, and all the dancers as well as my parents were expected to attend. Of course my father couldn't, but my mother had to represent him as head of the company, and so she stayed in the hospital until the last minute and then left for the dinner, permitting me to remain. My father now had twenty-four-hour nursing care, so I sat in the waiting room, somehow passing the night. I felt so helpless and scared, incapable of understanding how this could happen to my father, to me.

Since I could do nothing else to aid my father, I interlaced my fingers and began to pray. My ancestors had been Buddhist, but after the Communists took over China religion was rarely practiced openly, although it wasn't actually banned. In Canada, our family had begun to practice again on the occasional holiday, burning incense and praying to the Buddha. As for me, I had also grown up surrounded by the Christian holidays and traditions of our friends. I didn't know exactly to what or whom I was praying – perhaps it was to Buddha, to the Goddess of Mercy, to the saints, to everything good at once – but I prayed for my father to get through this, for him to wake up the next morning and recover. I was still praying when I fell asleep on the sofa. My mother woke me up – she had returned from the dinner – and sent me back to the hotel and a real bed, for tomorrow evening was our first performance.

I didn't want to dance. My father was in such critical condition, how could I even think of dancing? But the company was small and there was nobody to replace me. Deep down I knew that my father would have insisted I perform. The theater was very large, with perhaps three thousand seats, and the applause seemed to come from far away. Each time I entered the stage I thought, *Just dance for Dad, just dance to make his name live and to make him proud.* Afterwards, I could hardly remember dancing at all. As soon as the performance was over I rushed to the hospital again, and nobody knew that all the time I was praying inside for him to get better.

We had two more shows in Beijing and then had to begin the tour. My father's condition was still uncertain, and the specialist hadn't yet decided if he needed surgery. My mother would stay with him, but couldn't I stay too? I managed to convince the company to change the program for the first city on the tour so that I could stay in Beijing for three more days, just so that I could see my father get a little better. And I did hear him talk a little before leaving to join the others.

With my father ill and my mother at his side, the management of the tour fell onto Che's shoulders. Without my father's strong leadership presence, the dancers began to argue among themselves and propose

With Dad at a local newspaper's photo studio. He has always been a great support and inspiration to me.

With my dad at the Prix de Lausanne in 1986.

changes in the program. With the artistic director absent, suddenly everybody wanted a say in the decisions. Che struggled to maintain control, even as he rushed to the next theater, got the lighting set properly, attended official receptions. I wanted him to be able to count on me, and after dancing in the show each night I helped him with scheduling, casting, and other details. The tour turned out to be a success for the company and an intense learning experience for me, not only because of performing almost every night, but because of the turmoil within the company.

It lasted three or four weeks and then, while everyone else headed back to Vancouver, I rejoined my mother and father. I was relieved to discover Dad more like himself, talking and even walking about the ward. Still, he was very weak, and he would easily become short of breath. The doctor said his condition was stable but that my father would have to make major diet and lifestyle changes. For one thing, he had to give up his heavy smoking – and he did, never lighting a cigarette again. For another, he had to slow down his way of life and should never be put under stress. Only later would we consider what that meant for the Goh Ballet Company.

When the doctor said my father could travel, the Canadian Embassy helped us to get tickets on the day we wanted to leave. And so we departed Beijing, my father in first class to make him more comfortable. It was a strange feeling arriving home again. We had been away for almost two months and, while everything about the house was the same, everything was different — just the way our apartment in China felt when my father emigrated before us. My father's condition — in the next years he would have five arteries replaced in bypass surgery — meant great changes in his life. He had been working like Superman, running the company, teaching at the school, choreographing, giving master classes in other cities. Suddenly he had to stop everything, only gradually resuming some of his former occupations. My mother had to reorganize the school. As for the Goh Ballet Company, my father's ambitions came to an end. In time it was transformed into the Goh Ballet Training Company, a troupe for graduates of the school to gain experience by performing in school tours and other venues before turning professional. This made it a valuable addition to the school's training program and provided a next stage for graduates like myself. But it ended the possibility of the company becoming a professional home for me. I was going to have to dance somewhere else.

CHAPTER 8

TURNING PRO

Meanwhile, I had to finish high school. I had taken two years by correspondence in order to spend more time on dance, but my mother thought it might be good for me to get back to regular school again for my last year. She found out that a school just blocks from our house offered a half-day program for high achievers, and so I went to school in the mornings and continued my training in the afternoons. I also continued to study the major examination syllabus of the Royal Academy of Dance in London, and went on to perform for an examiner and adjudicators to earn the Solo Seal Award.

It seemed as if life was becoming stable again, when illness once more struck our family, illness that would prove tragic. My uncle Choo San, the choreographer with the Washington Ballet, became seriously ill. Before long he had to be hospitalized. Because of his own still delicate condition, my father couldn't go to New York to visit his younger brother. What was more difficult was keeping Choo San's illness a secret from his mother, who had moved back to Singapore; the family decided that she would not be able to bear such traumatic news

As Princess Florine in the Bluebird pas de deux from The Sleeping Beauty.

about her youngest and favorite child. My father found keeping the truth from his mother when they spoke or wrote emotionally difficult to endure (she never did find out before her own passing away). And then Uncle Choo San died. He was only thirty-eight, an innovative choreographer and a great interpreter of music who would have continued to grow artistically if his career had not been cut short.

❧

I knew that I would have to begin making career decisions but I was reluctant to give up being a student and turn professional. I felt that there was still so much more for me to learn. Perhaps, too, I was a little afraid of growing up. It was easier to focus my immediate attention on another competition.

As he slowly recuperated, my father began to do a little coaching. Together we decided that I should enter the Adeline Genée Competition in London, England, the same one that I had watched before entering the Prix de Lausanne. It was a prestigious international competition, associated with the Royal Academy of Dance (R.A.D.), and doing well could help me enter a professional career. I had to prepare two solos, and this time I was not in such a dizzy rush. On the other hand, unlike competing at the Prix, I now had higher expectations for myself.

One of the solos I chose was the White Swan variation from Act II of *Swan Lake*, a very slow, or adagio, solo. To a non-dancer it might appear that dancing fast is the most difficult, but in an adagio variation it takes tremendous control and strength to keep oneself precisely posed and to prevent oneself from faltering or losing balance. My father was now strong enough to travel, and both he and my mother came to London with me, where all the dancers spent the first week rehearsing and being coached by teachers from the R.A.D. Although some wonderful dancers from South Africa and Australia had come to the competition, I secretly hoped that I had a real chance for the gold medal. The final judging took place at the London Palladium Theatre and, as I prepared to do my White Swan variation, I felt weirdly unsure of myself and my balance. Yet once on stage I somehow struck some beautiful balances; they felt like an out-of-body experience, as if I were dancing with the aid of some magical force. I could only think, *Thank you, God, for helping me.*

After everyone had performed we waited for the three winners to be announced. First came the bronze medalist. Then the silver, and I heard the name "Chan Hon Goh" announced. Rising to receive my medal, I felt remarkably calm and even a little disappointed, since I had hoped for the gold, a sign of my rising confidence and ambition. But I was the first Canadian to ever receive a silver medal in the competition's history. I knew that it was a great achievement and could only help me as I began to search for the next stage in my career.

Not just in my career, but life. Although I was still a teenager, Che and I had been together for three years. I knew with certainty that I loved him and that he was the only man for me. One day he came home and showed me a diamond that he had bought, along with its certificate. "I'm going to design you a ring," he said, and I knew he meant an engagement ring. Three weeks later he gave the ring to me, a combination of white and yellow gold with an impression of a dove on the band to symbolize peace. And so we were engaged. We were in no rush to get married, especially since I was young, and as time went on it didn't seem to matter all that much since we began to feel as if we were married. We got teased sometimes about how long our engagement lasted – it would be almost ten years before we finally married – but Che and I had the confidence to do things our own way.

With the school year moving on, I could not avoid the question of what to do. The Goh Ballet was no longer a possibility and Vancouver had no major ballet company to join. But I was a homebody who was closely attached to her family and the things she knew. It took my father's friend and partner, Willy Tsao, who ran his own dance company in Hong Kong, to state the obvious. "You have to leave Vancouver," he said during a visit. "That is the only way to become a professional and

*With
Rex
Harrington
in
Madame
Butterfly.*

grow as a dancer." They were difficult words for me to hear, but I knew that he was right. I had no choice but to leave home.

But maybe I didn't have to go too far. The Pacific Northwest Ballet was a big company, and it was just a three-hour drive from British Columbia to Seattle in Washington State. I wrote a letter to the artistic directors, flashing my Prix de Lausanne and Adeline Genée awards and asking that they consider me for a soloist position. This was a slightly crazy thing to do: a young dancer was expected to begin in the corps de ballet (which is like the chorus) and only after several years, if she was deemed worthy, might she be promoted to the position of second soloist. A few years later she might be fortunate enough to become a first soloist. And after a few more years she might, if she were one of the chosen few, a dancer of star quality, be named a principal dancer, a prima ballerina.

So it was impertinent of me to ask for a soloist position. The artistic directors of the Pacific Northwest Ballet were a little taken aback by my bold request, but they asked me to come and take a class with the company. I took the bus alone to Seattle. Kent Stowell, one of the artistic directors, took me aside after class. "I can see that you have great potential, Chan," he said. "But it isn't realistic to ask us to make you a soloist. Besides, you aren't an American citizen and it would be tough to get you a work visa. I think you should get some more experience and then come back to us."

I returned to Vancouver a little wiser. I still felt that I did not want a corps position, but I knew that I wasn't ready to be a soloist. More training seemed to be the answer. The winter high-school semester passed, and when spring arrived I headed to New York, accompanied by my mother, to audition for the School of American Ballet. One of the best ballet schools in America, it was connected to the New York City Ballet, the great company dominated by the vision and choreography of George Balanchine. In the past, my mother had taken me to New York for a couple of week-long training sessions at the school, and now I decided to try for acceptance in their full one-year program after I finished high school.

The audition went just as well as I had hoped, and the Russian women who ran the school offered me a full scholarship for the year as well as an allowance of $400 a month. I was excited at the possibility, for I had an intense respect for these great teachers and a hunger to learn all I could from them. The only problem was that New York was such an expensive city that $400 would not be enough for an apartment, food, and whatever else I needed to survive. My parents were willing to give me all they could, but I knew how hard they worked and what a strain it would be on their finances. So I decided to apply for a grant from the Canada Council.

The Canada Council, the federal government's arts funding organization, had already awarded me a substantial grant the previous year to help prepare for the Adeline Genée Competition. I would have to do another live audition, and the Council paid to fly me to Toronto. Before leaving, a Canada Council administrator had spoken to me on the telephone. "You're graduating high school," he said. "Shouldn't you also consider auditioning for a professional company?"

"Well," I hesitated, "I guess I should. But I just thought I needed one more year of training." I didn't want to mention my desire to make a leap of progress so that I could avoid joining the corps of a company.

"Since you're going to Toronto, perhaps you might audition for the National Ballet of Canada," the administrator said. "Do you want to take a class with the company? You can see what the directors think."

So I agreed, although more reluctantly than the administrator could imagine. I flew alone to Toronto, and on Sunday I danced my audition for the Canada Council. Unknown to me at the time, one of the jury members was a man named James Kudelka. Then the resident choreographer of Les Grand Ballets Canadiens, he was a former dancer with the National Ballet. Privately, he thought as he watched me that I would be a good dancer for the National with its full repertoire. Neither he nor I could know that one day he would offer and create for me some of the most challenging roles of my career.

The next day I had my audition for the National Ballet of Canada.

The National Ballet of Canada was the country's largest company, with fifty or more dancers to perform the great story ballets of the 19th century in lavish productions. It also had its own orchestra, costume and set departments, management, and volunteer committees — in other words, it was a very large organization. Its Toronto home was the vast O'Keefe Centre (later to be renamed the Hummingbird Centre), but the company also toured across Canada and sometimes internationally as well. Like any major arts company, it had its share of triumphs, controversies, and funding crises. It also had stars – Karen Kain, Veronica Tennant, and Frank Augustyn – who had become beloved figures in Canada, although all of them by then were in the last years of their dancing careers.

The story ballets were the most popular with audiences, along with the annual Christmas production of *The Nutcracker*, but the National also programmed more recent and new works by Canadian and international choreographers, stretching the experience of the dancers as well as the audience. But Erik Bruhn, the artistic director who had brought in a lot of these modern works and had infused the company with a new energy, had died suddenly in 1986. Since then the National had been led by two people – Valerie Wilder and Lynn Wallis – with choreographer Glen Tetley as artistic associate, who were trying to maintain Erik Bruhn's vision during this period of transition. It was for the two women I had to audition.

I did not know even this much about the company when I arrived at the rehearsal studios in a handsome building near Toronto's theatre district called St. Lawrence Hall. I had no idea of how to recognize either Valerie Wilder or Lynn Wallis. A receptionist led me to the dressing room where I changed. I then joined the class, but there appeared to be nobody sitting in front to observe. Perhaps, I thought, they had forgotten about my audition. During center work a woman did come in and sit down, and a short time later a woman who was standing at the barre near me went to sit with her. I didn't know who was who (the first turned out to be Valerie Wilder, the second Lynn Wallis, both former dancers), but I knew they were there to watch me.

Class ended and the dancers began talking and gathering up their things. The woman who had sat down first came up to me and said, "Why don't we give you a few minutes to get changed. You can meet us upstairs in the office." I hurriedly dressed and made my way upstairs where Valerie and Lynn introduced themselves "We've heard a lot about you," said Valerie. "We even saw a report of your winning the silver medal at the Adeline Genée Competition."

"Your audition has convinced us you would do well in the company," said Lynn. "In fact, there is an immediate opening in the corps."

The offer did not thrill me as much as they naturally expected it to. I still had a strong interest in attending the School of American Ballet and, besides, the position was in the corps. I flew back to Vancouver, unsure of what to do. Shortly after my return, a letter arrived from Valerie Wilder. She wrote that the National Ballet of Canada was offering me a contract as a corps de ballet member beginning in the middle of June. But the letter also stated that she saw in me the potential to rise quickly through the ranks of the company. I knew that she was telling me I wouldn't remain in the corps for long. It wasn't a guarantee – every dancer has to prove herself over and over again – but it gave me the expectation I needed to overcome my reservations.

So nervously, I signed the contract. I would now become a member of the National Ballet of Canada. Many new dancers to the National came up through its own school, but for me joining the company meant working with directors and ballet masters and other dancers who were all strangers to me. No longer would I have the security of studying with my father and mother, and working with dancers I had known for years at the Goh Ballet. And it meant that Che and I would be separated for a year before he could come. I would be alone in a city twice as large as Vancouver, four thousand kilometers from everything I knew.

Was I ready? Well, I would just have to find out. I certainly felt that, once I had made up my mind to join, I was ready to do my best. Along with my fears and reservations was an even stronger determination to prove my worth. Just as the young girl had needed to show that she could do well in school, so did the suddenly grown-up woman need to prove that she could succeed. Besides, I wanted to get out of the corps. Only then would I really be able to dance.

PHOTO GALLERY

As Juliet in John Cranko's Romeo and Juliet.

With Ryan Boorne in James Kudelka's Cruel World.

With Aleksandar Antonijevic in "Diamonds" from George Balanchine's Jewels.

Living a fairy tale, from the ballroom scene of Ben Stevenson's Cinderella.

From James Kudelka's The Four Seasons, *the Spring pas de deux with Rex Harrington.*

With Geon van der Wyst in James Kudelka's Swan Lake.

As the Sylph in Erik Bruhn's La Sylphide.

As Cio-Cio San in Stanton Welch's Madame Butterfly.

Kitri solo in Act I of Don Quixote.

In Act I of Peter Wright's Giselle.

As the Swan Queen in Act IV of Erik Bruhn's Swan Lake.

The finale of "Diamonds" from Jewels.

ONE OF THE CORPS

Che accompanied me to Toronto, although he would have to return to Vancouver after two weeks to fulfill his teaching and choreographic obligations. Family friends had helped me find a condominium in Toronto's Market Square, just two minutes away from the St. Lawrence Hall where the National rehearsed. But as the condo wasn't ready, we had to stay for the first two weeks in an apartment hotel that the company had found for us. We arrived two days before my first work day, and our friends Flora and Chia Seng toured us around the city and took us out for dinner. I made sure to go to bed early that Sunday night so as to be ready in the morning for my first class.

Taking class does not end for a dancer once she becomes a professional. Every work day begins with a class of an hour and fifteen minutes, in part to act as a warm-up, but also because dancers must constantly work to improve their mastery of the steps and increase their wide vocabulary of movement. So I got up and, with the television on as soothing background noise, I sat at the kitchen table while Che made me a couple of pieces of toast. *Who would teach the class?* I wondered,

What other dancers would attend? And afterwards? I knew that the company was going to be doing the ballet *Onegin*, a very dramatic and emotionally complex ballet set in 19th century Russia and choreographed by John Cranko. No one had told me what minor part I was to dance or when the rehearsals would be. I hadn't known enough to ask beforehand for a copy of the schedule.

Sitting at the kitchen table, I suddenly began to tremble. It felt very strange, as if the blood were draining from my body. I turned to Che and said quietly, "I'm . . . not feeling . . . well."

He looked at me and I saw the panic on his face. "You've turned pale," he said. "Are you all right?"

"No, I don't feel good."

And then everything turned white.

The anxiety of my first day had caused me to pass out. I knew nothing more until I heard Che calling my name and felt his hand on my face. He must have carried me to the bedroom where I was now lying. How much time had passed? An hour? No, only a minute. But I felt as if I had just awoken from a wonderfully refreshing nap. I sat up, feeling absolutely fine, but poor Che was worried sick about me. "I should call an ambulance," he said.

I looked at the clock; it was almost nine. "I've got to go."

"You're not going to go now!"

"But I'm fine." I got up from the bed, feeling brand new. I put up my hair and Che accompanied me on the subway and the short street-car ride through the sweltering June heat to the St. Lawrence Hall. We said good-bye, Che still worried, and a secretary showed me where to change. To my surprise, the dressing room was very cramped. The other dancers were talking among themselves, but I just found a corner to myself. I went to the studio where the women's class was being held. As I was early, I started to warm up at the barre while more people came in, none of whom I recognized.

As frivolous Olga in Onegin, *with Sally-Ann Hickin (left) and Lisa Jones (right).*

After the class, the director's assistant called a short meeting and introduced me and three other young dancers to the rest of the company. The dancers began coming up to welcome us. From the assistant I had found out my role in *Onegin* — a girlfriend of Tatiana, the main character — and what my rehearsal schedule was. After class I worked with a ballet mistress, Lorna Geddes, one of the original members of the company from the early 1950s, who showed me the steps for my role. It wasn't a difficult part, but I had some interaction with the principal female dancer, and I was happy to be in a real story ballet. The day turned out to be short and I was done by mid-afternoon, when Che met me and we began to walk home. On the way he said smiling, "Chan, stop dancing in the street," and I realized that I was going over the steps of the choreography as we walked.

During the next two weeks, I rehearsed more. I had some partnering in the second act of the ballet. The male dancer was also new and far less experienced than the Chinese partners I had danced with in the Goh Ballet Company. It can be frustrating to work with a partner who is hesitant or unsure about lifting or catching or supporting you, and who doesn't give you the confidence you need to do your own best.

Learning this first role did not change my mind about wanting to move up from the corps as soon as possible. I could see that corps dancers worked hard, sometimes even harder than the principals, and that their roles could be equally stressful. But while some dancers might be satisfied in the corps or even as a soloist – with more interesting parts but still without the responsibility of leading the company or having the success of the whole performance depend on her individual perform-ance – I simply could not. My goal of one day becoming a principal dancer became even more unshakable, and I thought that if I did not reach the top I would be a failure. Even learning this first small role meant a great deal, because I felt that management would be watching me closely and judging whether I deserved to move up. I would have to prove myself.

The two weeks of rehearsal were a particularly anxious and exciting time for two reasons. For me personally, everything was new. I was con-stantly afraid of missing a rehearsal or showing up at the wrong studio – the company had four studios in two different buildings, and it wasn't always clear from the schedule which dancers were in which scenes. Also, I was trying to fit into the new company, making my first tenta-tive contact with other young dancers but still feeling lost and friendless as just one small person in a huge organization. But the whole company was also expectant; we were about to leave for a short season at Lincoln Center in New York City.

New York was to me the dance capital of North America. It seemed a wonderful, if frightening, stroke of luck that my debut with the National Ballet of Canada should take place there. The production team and crew had to prepare the set and scenery, the costumes had to be readied, even the orchestra had to prepare. At the Goh Ballet, I was used to dancing to taped music, not the playing of real musicians. And then the day of departure arrived and I found it intimidating just to gather with the other dancers in the airport. We all stood in a loose group while the company manager called out our last names to give us our tickets. When he called out "Goh," one of the male dancers shouted,

"Goh–gone!" making everybody laugh and me blush with embarrassment. The dancer was Rex Harrington, a young principal dancer who I had decided was the best male dancer in the company and who was already partnering Karen Kain a good deal. But that was the first time he had ever directed a remark towards me.

And so I arrived in New York – age nineteen, a dancer with the National Ballet of Canada, about to make my debut on the stage of the Metropolitan Opera House at Lincoln Center. And I was absolutely homesick. My parents and Che were back in Canada; Vancouver seemed so far away; I was surrounded by people who were supposed to be my fellow artists but were virtual strangers to me. We were scheduled to take our classes in the studios at the Met. Walking in, I saw the wonderful dancer Natalia Makarova, who was our guest artist for the season, at one end of the barre, and the spectacular ABT dancer Fernando Bujones chatting with some other dancers nearby. Of course I remembered coming to New York with my parents and my late uncle, Choo San, who had taken us backstage. How long ago that seemed! Despite my loneliness, I could not help being thrilled that my dream of dancing on the stage of the Metropolitan Opera was coming true.

The season in New York went well for the company, and my sense that management was watching my performances must have been true. Towards the end of the week, a cast list for the company's upcoming Ontario Place program was posted and I had been chosen to dance the first solo from *La Bayadère*, a role that had in fact been promised me by Valerie Wilder in her letter offering me a position in the company. Two second soloists would dance the part as well, the three of us alternating nights, as is customary. It was an exotic ballet set in India and in this scene, The Kingdom of the Shades, the prince imagines that he sees the beautiful temple dancer Nikiya, who has been murdered. He sees a row of dancers, all of whom look like Nikiya, and then three dancers in turn perform solos, each of which represents an aspect of her personality. My solo was quick and precise, with a lot of hops on pointe, the most playful and effervescent of the three. Everyone in the company was surprised by the casting and a few eyebrows went up, especially from corps dancers who had been with the National longer than I had. Their reaction was understandable, for a ballet company is a very competitive environment. On one level, the members of a company act as if they are a large family; certainly they spend as much time together as any family does. But underneath the warmth, other more difficult emotions simmer. Every dancer constantly wonders what management thinks of her dancing, and whether she will get a good role or be promoted to the next level. And the other dancers around her, who are supposed to be her friends, are also her competitors. This is just one of the many stresses that a dancer lives under every day. No wonder emotions can run high, and unhappy dancers, feeling as if they are not valued enough, sometimes decide to leave a company.

Every year the National held free summer performances of short works and excerpts from longer ballets at Ontario Place, a waterfront park in Toronto with an outdoor theater. These shows were a way to bring attention to the upcoming fall season, acting as a public showcase for the talents and repertoire of the company. As I was soon to discover, there is almost never enough time to rehearse, and even while we were still in New York I had to begin learning my solo. My coach was Magdalena Popa, the principal ballet mistress who was responsible for rehearsing all the principal dancers and some of the soloists. After just a couple of rehearsals she picked up on the same weaknesses that my father had been trying to correct in me and that I always had to be reminded about. In any company a dancer is at the mercy of a coach, who can choose how much she wants to give, and I am thankful for Magdalena's help in making me a better dancer. Later Magdalena would guide me through virtually every major role I performed with the company.

We returned to Toronto. Besides the solo, I had a corps de ballet role to perform in *La Bayadère* in the shows when another dancer had the solo. Most of the other seventeen dancers already knew the corps choreography so the second soloist taught it to me. I had a difficult time in rehearsals using my peripheral vision to match my own placement – a little too much to one side or another would ruin the pattern – within the line of dancers. Nor did I like having to worry about, say, placing my hand at the same level every time to be in exact coordination with the others. Dancers who had come up through the National Ballet School would have had some corps training, but I had done more solo and pas de deux work instead. I kept thinking, *How am I supposed to dance well if I have to worry about such things?* To me it felt like dancing in a cage. So all the time that I was trying hard to fit in, deep down I felt that this was not what dancing meant to me.

During the week before Ontario Place, I came down with what I thought was the flu, my stomach in such turmoil that I could hardly keep down food. I began to feel weak and dehydrated. Only later did I realize that it was nerves.

The night of the first performance came. We warmed up on the open-air stage while families that had come early laid out their picnic meals on the grass. Kids with posters shyly approached Karen Kain for autographs. The informal setting took a little of the pressure off, but I could still feel my own excitement building at the thought of performing in the National's home town – my own new home. Before long the surrounding slopes were crowded with people, among them my parents, who had flown in from Vancouver to see me.

My solo came off well. Afterwards, my parents came up to congratulate me. My flu symptoms had mysteriously disappeared, and I said to them, "Let's go out to eat. I'm famished."

During my first year in the company, I learned a great deal by watching. Whenever I could, I watched the principals rehearse and take class, admiring Karen Kain's beautiful footwork and musicality, Veronica Tennant's acting ability, Yoko Ichino's strong technique and coordination,

and Kimberly Glasco's beautiful ballerina quality. It seemed to me that all the prima ballerinas breathed a purer air. I watched the men too — Frank Augustyn, Rex Harrington, Raymond Smith, Gregory Osborne, and Owen Montague — and saw how individual were their styles.

In some dance companies there is an overly competitive, "glass-in-your-pointe-shoe" attitude among the members. But at the National the other dancers were mostly friendly and helpful. During my first fall season we toured the Maritime provinces, and I came across Karen Kain in the change room of the hotel gym. She said to me, "I just want to tell you that everything you're doing on stage and in class is so right. It's wonderful to see, and don't ever lose it." I was grateful for her words, not just for the encouragement but because of how lost I was still feeling. The company still felt like a massive organization and I just one small dancer, and I couldn't help contrasting the feeling with the individual attention that all of us had received as part of the Goh Ballet Company. Perhaps it was because of feeling so close to my family —

along with my upbringing with its values of politeness and modesty, and my own natural shyness – but I had real trouble making close friends or feeling as if I belonged to a group. Touring was particularly difficult for me, because I often felt alone and even dreaded the days off when I rarely knew what to do with myself.

As for the dancing, we were doing a mixed program and I had both demi-soloist and corps work to do. The only real unfriendliness I encountered was with the older corps dancers, twenty-five or twenty-six years old, who had been with the company for a few years but were not being given any solos. As a result of their own frustrations, they couldn't help being a little impatient with me as I learned the corps work. And despite my difficulty in matching the other dancers, I found the steps themselves technically unchallenging and too often more mechanical than artistic. Corps members don't get individual coaching, and I had always liked one-on-one attention from a teacher to refine my technique and style. After a while I began to worry that my technique was slipping. And how does an ambitious young dancer stand out in the corps when the whole object is to blend in? How could management see my potential and give me more solo work?

When I joined the National, the company had been searching for a new artistic director for some time. I did not think about how important the choice would be for me and all the other dancers, but the simple truth is that any dancer's career is in the palm of the director's hand. Large ballet companies are run in a traditional manner – the artistic director is like a king who makes decrees and hands them to the dancers. He decides, sometimes in consultation with other members of the artistic staff, not only the repertoire but also which dancers will dance which parts. We dancers have little if any choice in the matter. I am not against this approach; an artistic director with a strong vision can make a great company. But any dancer needs to feel that the director understands and appreciates her talent.

Our new artistic director turned out to be Reid Anderson. Although from New Westminster, British Columbia, he had spent years as a principal dancer at the renowned Stuttgart Ballet in Germany, and he had already worked with the National by staging for them their first production of *Onegin*. In fact, I had seen Reid Anderson himself dance the lead in *Onegin* when I was just a kid, and he knew my father because the two of them had taught at the Banff School of Fine Arts. I had met Reid for the first time when I was preparing for the Adeline Genée Competition. My father invited Reid, who was then director of Ballet B.C., to watch me rehearse. I didn't know how his appointment to the National Ballet might affect my own career. But it was Reid Anderson who would really see my ability and pull me out of the corps.

Once again summer came around and, with it, our open-air performances at Ontario Place. It had been some time since I had any challenging dancing to do, but when I checked the cast list I discovered that I had been named to dance the *Corsaire* pas de deux. One year my first solo, and the next my first partnering in a piece that required some virtuoso dancing. Reid Anderson had paired me, a corps member, with a principal dancer, Jeremy Ransom. Surely he was testing my dancing ability, both for technique and expressiveness, and perhaps also for professionalism under the spotlight. It was tremendously exciting, but equally daunting.

Jeremy and I had only about two weeks to prepare. The rehearsals were a struggle, as it seemed to me that Jeremy just wasn't a natural partner, as some fine male dancers aren't. Yet I was determined not to have the awful stomach troubles of the year before and I managed to keep calm. Our first show went wonderfully well. The movements seemed to flow without conscious effort, the timing was as natural as the beating of my heart, and the emotions came unbidden.

Afterwards, I went back to the corps dressing room. When someone knocked on the door, another dancer answered it and then came up to me.

"Reid wants to see you," she said.

I went out and Reid, waiting for me, put his arms around me and gave me a great hug. "I'm really, really glad to see what you did out there," he said. "I'm proud of you."

Somehow I managed to stumble out a reply. "Thank you for the opportunity to do this."

"Oh," he smiled, "there'll be more to come."

And so began the kind of support and affirmation that a dancer thrives on, that helps her to have the courage to grow. It was also true that, over time, I came to see that Reid perceived me as a certain kind of dancer – perfect for the classical "tutu" ballets and girlish roles. He did not cast me in other, more emotionally realistic parts. But Reid gave me the support that I needed to rise in the company.

So far, I had been featured only in mixed programs or excerpts, rather than in any of the full-length productions that most people associate with ballet. But I knew that in December the company would perform its annual season of *The Nutcracker* – the perennial favorite, especially with children – to the famous musical score by Tchaikovsky. The National's version, first choreographed by its founding artistic director Celia Franca, had been in the repertoire for decades (it would be replaced with a dazzling new version a few years later), and its characters – the mysterious Herr Drosselmeyer, Clara and Fritz (played by young student dancers), the toy soldiers who battle the mice – continued to enchant audiences. I was naturally curious to know what role Reid might think appropriate for me. Would I get one of the divertissements, the virtuoso dances in the second act, to perform – Marzipan or Spanish – or would I simply get more corps work and a few other tiny roles? Though I hoped for some nugget, I was amazed when the cast list went up and I saw my name next to two leading roles: the Snow Queen in Act I and the Sugar Plum Fairy in Act II.

My partner, Kevin Pugh, had danced his role for many years, but it was my first time leading the company in a full-length ballet. This sort of role was just what belonging to the National meant to me, and I was naturally thrilled. But perhaps the happiest moment of all occurred

during my debut performance when, as the Sugar Plum Fairy, I descended in the basket of a hot-air balloon and, looking out into the audience, saw my mother and father watching me with awe.

In a year and a half as a corps member of the National Ballet of Canada, I had been given the opportunity to dance solos, a pas de deux, and the leading roles in *The Nutcracker*. The management that hired me, and the director who followed, had been true to their word. They had given me opportunities to show that I deserved a more prominent position in the company. Che had finally joined me in Toronto, and I was no longer alone. I hardly felt satisfied. I sensed too much potential in myself, too much expressiveness hungering to get out. Nor was I fully at home yet, or even confident of my place. But I was full of hope and expectation and I was determined to make the most of every chance I got.

As the Sugar Plum Fairy in Celia Franca's production of The Nutcracker, *with Jeremy Ransom.*

CHAPTER 10

ॐ

ON THE RISE

It was under Reid Anderson that I rose from a member of the corps to principal dancer and began to dance the roles that I had long dreamed of. The rise was fairly quick and always steady, with Reid offering me new opportunities for growth without thrusting me into roles that I was not yet ready for.

In his first year at the National, Reid did not promote any of the dancers, but kept the company as it was until he had a chance to observe us all. During that time Veronica Tennant, an important star for the National, retired, and it came time to make some changes. In June 1990, two years after I began as a corps member, Reid called several dancers into his office, one at a time. I was one of those called and, when the door was closed, Reid told me that he was promoting me to second soloist. "You are going to lead the National in the future," he said. "You are going to be one of the stars of this company."

I was twenty-one and could not take in all that he meant, perhaps because beneath my confidence remained both self-doubt and a realistic sense of how much farther I still had to go. But I was ecstatic and

*In the
dressing room.*

hurried to tell Che. We both agreed that moving out of the corps into a soloist position was the biggest hurdle in a dancer's advancing career.

A dancer doesn't only need to improve her technical skills and artistic style as she rises to more prominent roles; she must also gain confidence on stage and develop the stamina, which was never my greatest attribute, needed to dance larger and more demanding roles. It was not until after I was promoted to first soloist in January 1992, a year and a half after becoming second soloist, that I got to play the Sylph in *La Sylphide*. First performed by the Royal Danish Ballet in 1836, *La Sylphide* is one of the great ballets of the high romantic period. The role of the Sylph – not human at all but a sort of otherworldly sprite or fairy – requires a dancer to be graceful and charming, and to appear lighter than air. In the story, a kind of tragic fairy tale, James, the lead male character, is about to be married but falls in love with the Sylph. He pursues her, only to be fooled by a witch who promises to help him win the Sylph's heart. Instead, he causes her death.

My debut in the role – with Jeremy Ransom as the male lead – was received by the critics in a way that showed how my concentration was still on the technical demands of a role. The *Globe and Mail* praised my "technical mastery," especially my "ability to freeze en pointe with absolute security, in a way that caught the breath." But the critic also wrote that the character was "as thin as tissue paper" and, even though he partly faulted the ballet, that criticism did sting a little. The reviewer for the *Toronto Sun* wrote of my "exquisite technique" but also claimed – horror! – that I had a "penchant for mugging." Well, it seemed true that my acting skills, which I had not fully concentrated on, had some way to go. In fact, I did not yet fully realize that although brilliant technique can impress an audience, it cannot move one. Only by bringing deep emotions to a role can a dancer make the audience really *feel*. At this point – I was all of twenty-two years old – I was still consumed with perfecting my technical skills.

I was so consumed that I sometimes pushed myself beyond healthy limits. In my third year at the National I began to get a pain in my left foot. Thinking – or at least hoping – that it would go away, I continued to take class, rehearse, and perform. But instead of it lessening, I began to get "referred" pain in other areas of my foot. The doctors couldn't zone in on the problem because of the different points that hurt, until finally an indentation began to form in my foot where the muscle wasn't receiving enough nutrients from the blood. Only then, six months later, did the doctors give me yet another bone scan and X-ray and conclude that I had a stress fracture in the metatarsal bone. Stress fractures are caused by excessive use and constant repetition of the same movement, the obvious result of overwork. Treatment: six weeks with no weight on the foot.

That meant six weeks without dancing, and so I had to go on sick leave. About the only exercise I could do without hurting my foot was swimming and Pilates. But it was a difficult time mentally more than physically, because without dancing I felt lost. Who was I without dance? Going to class or rehearsals and watching the others proved to be too painful, and I ended up going back to Vancouver with Che. Those six weeks seemed to last forever and, although the doctors reassured me I would get better, I was a little afraid that my dancing would never be the same. Eventually I was able to begin physiotherapy treatment and began gentle exercises, slowly increasing the weight on my foot.

As I healed, I came to see that this injury was teaching me a lesson. Pain is the body's way of sending you a warning message, and you had better not ignore it. Until now I had tried to command my body to obey my wishes, rather than listening to its needs. If I wanted a long career as a dancer, I had better respect my physical self and take care of it. That meant not only responding to pain, but also eating properly and getting enough rest in order to recuperate from the extreme exertion of dancing. It took another two stress fractures for this lesson to really sink in. Dancers face many difficulties; physical injuries are only one. The desire to excel, to look and perform beautifully, to conform to the so-called "ideal" appearance of a ballerina – all these pressures can take their toll. Some dancers suffer from stress, others develop eating disorders that can severely threaten their health. And while dance companies are now more aware of these dangers, dancers are still pretty much on their own. Those weeks of forced rest due to injury seemed like time lost from dancing that I would never recover, but in retrospect they were valuable in a different way. I knew that I would have to take care of myself, body and soul. If I didn't, I would never get to dance the great roles of the major ballets, roles that I was growing towards.

Despite the injuries, however, I was starting to feel more set-tled in life. Che and I were living together happily, and he was developing his own fine career as a teacher in the dance department of George Brown College. He was often invited to guest teach, both in Canada and abroad. One Saturday night I was speaking long-distance to my mother and suddenly mentioned to her that I had been thinking about getting a dog – we had two during my Vancouver years. To my surprise she encouraged the idea, and the next day I browsed through the classified section of the *Toronto Star*. And that was how we found Daly, an apricot miniature poodle, the oldest of his litter and just a little puffball when we brought him home. He cried for six weeks every moment he wasn't with us, making us hollow-eyed from lack of sleep, but he turned out to be one of the best things that ever happened to us. With Daly, both Che and I learned to be more considerate, responsible, and nurturing.

At home with Daly on his sofa.

On a wintry day in February 1993, the snow was falling over Front Street and I, always feeling the cold, was wrapped up like a bear, a warm hat pulled over my head. I crossed the street and went into the O'Keefe Centre where class was being held when I saw Reid Anderson. "Come in for a second," he said to me. "I want to see you in my office."

Still cold, I left my hat on. "Listen," Reid said. "I've just proposed to the board that I promote you to principal dancer. I want to do it at the start of our new season in July but I'm not sure if we have the budget. If I can't then, I'm going to do it in January of the following year."

Reid came through with his offer and I became a principal dancer in January 1994, the first principal dancer in the National Ballet's history to be of Chinese heritage. It was five years from joining the National Ballet of Canada as a corps member to becoming a principal dancer, so naturally I felt proud of my own rapid rise. And I was unsure – despite it having been my determined goal – of whether I really was good enough.

The proof, of course, would be in the dancing. I did not think that a dancer had really proved herself, could call herself a true ballerina, until she had danced all the leads in the major ballet repertoire. And so I was elated when Reid gave me a chance to dance my first *Sleeping Beauty*.

I had loved *Sleeping Beauty* since I was a kid, when I had seen videos of Natalia Makarova and my other favorite ballerina, Margot Fonteyn, in the role. Fonteyn was perhaps most famous for the role of Aurora, the beautiful princess who is pricked by a cursed needle and falls asleep for a hundred years before being awakened by the kiss of a prince. Many consider it to be the finest classical ballet of the 19th century, and the composer Tchaikovsky's greatest score. Back in Vancouver with my parents, I had seen the National on tour perform the famous Nureyev production, and now here I was at the age of twenty-four, about to dance in the same version.

Karen Kain would also be dancing the role of Aurora. In fact, the season would be her farewell to *Sleeping Beauty*. I was able to prepare not only with Magdalena Popa but also with Karen. Karen's partner, a guest dancer from the Paris Opera, would not arrive until a week before the performances began, and Karen liked to have company in the studio, so the two of us would rehearse together. She was very generous about offering advice and suggestions. Both she and Kimberly Glasco, who would also dance as Aurora at some performances, warned me about the famous rose adagio in the first act of the ballet. During this scene, four suitors arrive to ask for Aurora's hand in marriage, and each one offers

her a rose. Dancing with each in turn, Aurora performs a long prome-
nade, posed and balancing on one foot while the male dancer walks her
around. To the audience it is all light and beautiful, but for the dancer it
is an excruciatingly long time to stay on pointe. It demands both fine
precision and control, and Karen and Kimberly told me that my legs
would feel like tree trunks by the end. Fortunately, I didn't quite believe
them, because if I had known just how exhausting the scene was I
would have been defeated before ever starting. In fact, the whole ballet
was my first experience of how absolutely depleting a three-act ballet
could be.

The role had a lot of other challenges as well. At the beginning,
Aurora has to run down a long staircase for her birthday party, all youth-
ful effervescence. But it is no easy thing to run down stairs in pointe
shoes, while wearing a tutu that blocks the view of the steps. My
favorite part, however, was the Act III wedding scene, in which Aurora
comes down those stairs again, together with her prince, this time as a
mature woman ready to accept the throne. Tchaikovsky's music always
elevated me to a higher, grander place, and the scene culminates in a
grand pas de deux with the prince – a triumphant finish.

Unlike the somewhat mixed response to my debut in *La Sylphide*,
my performance in *Sleeping Beauty* received only praise. "A born Aurora
if there ever was one," wrote the *Globe and Mail*. The reviewer even compared me to Margot Fonteyn! "With her light, easy jump, her playful
musicality, her elegant line and her daring balances, she's already an Aurora
to remember." For me, it was not merely a step but a leap forward.

Despite its challenges, *Sleeping Beauty* seemed a natural ballet for me.
The next time I got to dance as Aurora, it was with Vladimir Malakhov,
one of the greatest classical dancers of our time. Certainly it felt more
natural than the next one – *Swan Lake*. *Swan Lake* is the best known
classical ballet, and the image of the ballerina as swan has become one
of the few ballet images to enter the popular imagination. It is a kind of
fairy tale, but also a tragedy, in which Odette the Swan Queen can
return to human form only when a man promises to love her faithfully.

With Vladimir Malakhov, after the last curtain call of Sleeping Beauty.

Prince Siegfried falls in love with her but is tricked by the evil enchanter Von Rothbart to believe that his daughter Odile, the Black Swan, is Odette. When Siegfried mistakenly declares his intention to marry Odile, he dooms the Swan Queen. In the end, Siegfried throws himself into the lake and drowns.

Performing as both Odette and Odile is a challenge both to the endurance and to the acting ability of the ballerina. My coach insisted on the strictest technical precision in this, Erik Bruhn's version of the ballet. The first weeks of rehearsal were particularly difficult, especially learning the White Swan part in Act II, slow and sustained. I almost began to feel as if I didn't know how to do a single ballet step correctly. Things eventually got better, but I continued to feel constrained, as if I were dancing with the style of the coach instead of my own. My first performance was a matinee, or afternoon performance, and I don't know whether my shoes were too tight or I hadn't warmed up enough – or maybe I had just been trying too hard and had over-exerted myself

in the first entrance, causing my muscles to cramp up – but just before going back on stage for the White Swan solo I thought to myself, *I cannot feel my feet.* They had gone absolutely numb. How could I go out there and dance the solo? Standing in the wing, the cygnets' dance coming to an end on the stage, I pounded my feet on the floor, trying to get some feeling in them. When that didn't work I used my fists on my calves. Nothing. All I could do was go out there. Fortunately, my muscles remembered the steps even if I couldn't feel my feet, and I got through the solo. But it was a very scary feeling and I was relieved it did not occur again during the run.

My favorite act of the ballet was the fourth, with its tragic depth of feeling – so different from the happy triumph I felt at the end of *Sleeping Beauty* – and as the performances went on I was able to lose myself in the role more and more. Dancing the last act I felt a great sadness, as if something had been stolen from my soul, an emptiness where love had once been. Taking the curtain calls, I felt almost subdued rather than the elation I had felt after *Sleeping Beauty.*

❦

It was easy for an artistic director to see me in roles such as the Sylph, or Aurora, or the White Swan. All of them lend themselves to a dancer with lyrical qualities, fine technique, and a delicate appearance – qualities that the critics praised me for. But I wanted to play other roles too, characters with even deeper emotional lives, that would require me to grow as an artist and not just technically. So when it was announced that the National would revive its production of *Giselle* for the next season, I desperately hoped that Reid would choose me as one of the principals to dance the title role.

It was just before our summer break, when the company would disband until rehearsals in the fall. One day Reid called me into his office; I arrived to find the ballet mistress, Magdalena, there as well. "Well, Chan," Reid said, "I feel that we should talk before the break. I've been very, very happy with your dancing and I can tell that it comes

As the Black Swan Odile in Erik Bruhn's version of Swan Lake, *right before the Prince is tricked into pledging his love.*

from the heart. Now I'm trying to decide on *Giselle* and I'm not worried about your being able to dance it. But I'm not convinced that you can do the acting necessary."

Reid went on. "Of course you know there's the famous mad scene in the first act." I could only nod. "That's ten minutes without steps but just acting. I'm not convinced you're ready for that. I'm going to think about it over the break. I haven't decided, but I wanted you to know what's on my mind."

I thanked Reid for his directness and then left hurriedly, knowing that tears were about to flow. It just crushed my heart to hear him say those words – crushed me because I too had the same doubts. When a person fears that something is true, it hurts even more. I felt upset for days. I didn't know if I had the ability, and yet I wanted so much to have it.

Giselle is a French masterpiece, renowned for both its romantic dance movements and for being a story of betrayal and eternal love. The dashing Count Albrecht dresses as an ordinary villager and falls in love with Giselle. Despite Giselle's mother's warnings, she succumbs to Albrecht and falls in love too. But when she finds out that he is really a count and already engaged to be married, Giselle loses her reason out of grief. In the mad scene, she imagines her meetings with Albrecht over again and, dancing in her madness, dies of a broken heart. In Act II, the queen of the Wilis, who are ghosts of young women, calls Giselle from the grave and commands her to goad Albrecht into dancing to exhaustion and death. But instead, Giselle's pure love gives Albrecht strength. As dawn breaks and Giselle melts away, Albrecht is left alive, though in deep sorrow.

I was truly beginning to understand that technical skill, while absolutely required, was only the basis upon which to express a character. Like an actor, a dancer has to find within herself the emotional truths of a character. She has to move beyond the dance. Just as a good dancing coach can help, so can an acting coach, and I spent the summer taking private acting lessons. Then in July, wanting to give myself a

My Toronto
debut as Giselle
(with Nicholas Khan).

symbol of freedom and change, I impulsively had my long hair cut short, for the first time since I became an adult.

In August, I returned to work with the other members of the company. When the casting sheet for *Giselle* went up, I saw my name – I would be one of the principals to dance the role! Reid had changed his mind. Perhaps he still wasn't sure, but he was going to give me a chance. My first feeling was of pure joy, and my second sudden dismay that I had cut off my long hair.

During rehearsal I was encouraged to overcome my reticence during the mad scene, to really let go and use my eyes, my facial expressions, my arm gestures to reveal all that Giselle is experiencing. Meanwhile, the wig department had to fit me with a wig that I would wear over my short hair.

Before performing in Toronto, the company took the ballet on a tour of western Canada. My first performance was before an audience of students in Saskatoon, and I felt afterwards that I had done all right. Our next stop was Winnipeg, where I wasn't scheduled to perform. But I rehearsed at the Royal Winnipeg Ballet, and there I saw Evelyn Hart. Evelyn and I went back a long way, to her first private classes with my father when I was still a kid. She had always been generous and supportive, so it felt natural for me to ask her about the role. Evelyn took me out to dinner where she spoke at length on character development and especially on connecting with my partner. And because she was actively dancing, I could ask her detailed questions about certain steps and crucial moments.

My second performance was before a regular audience in Victoria. After the show I returned to my hotel room and sat on the edge of the bed. My performance had been technically polished, I had held all my balances, but still there was an element of emotion within the character that I hadn't fully released, a connection I hadn't made. I started to cry and could not stop, just sitting with my shoulders shaking and the tears streaming down my face. Only later did I understand that certain depths of characterization cannot be found in the rehearsal studio, but only through the process of performing over and over before an audience.

From Victoria we went on to Vancouver. My father and mother came for the performance, as well as lots of students from the Goh Ballet Academy. Many of my old Vancouver friends came too. The local television stations showed up to capture the home-town girl who had made good. But the additional pressure was balanced by having now performed the role twice. This time, when I went on stage, I forgot about the technical aspects, about how long I held my balances, and truly lost myself in being Giselle. Taking the curtain calls, I felt absolutely drained, but also as if a great emotional weight were lifting away from me.

When I came off stage Reid was waiting for me. "I'm glad I was wrong," he said.

As I grew into the role, Giselle would become one of my favorite roles in the repertoire.

CHAPTER II

MORE CHALLENGES

Although I was now in my twenties, I still felt a lot of the little girl in me. When we went on tour I sometimes felt lonely or even lost, just as I had when my father left us behind in Beijing. Although I had reached my goal of becoming a principal dancer, I still felt the need to prove myself, and to please all the people around me – the artistic director and the ballet mistress, my mother and father when they came to watch one of my shows, Che, and of course the audience. I was rarely satisfied with my own performances, and I was always looking towards the next challenge.

Just before a show at the O'Keefe Centre in November 1995, Karen Kain came onstage to announce that Reid Anderson had decided to step down from his position of artistic director. He was going to return to the Stuttgart Ballet in Germany and take on the same role there.

I knew that with change can come new opportunities. The new artistic director, James Kudelka, had begun his career as a dancer at the National but had left the company to become a choreographer, making dances for Les Grands Ballets Canadiens, the Joffrey Ballet, the American

Not acting, but becoming Tatiana in Onegin.

Ballet Theatre, and the San Francisco Ballet, as well as for us at the National. My first encounter with him, as he would later remind me, had occurred years before when I auditioned for the Canada Council and he had been on the jury. This would be the first time that the artistic director of the National Ballet of Canada would also be a major choreographer, able to create his own versions of the classic repertoire as well as totally new dances.

We dancers had to adapt to his approach and style. He gave us new dancing opportunities that we otherwise would not have had. Soon after he took over, it was announced that we would be reviving *Onegin*. As a corps member I had played the small part of a girlfriend; later as a soloist I had taken on the character of Olga, Tatiana's frivolous younger sister. But this time I wanted to play Tatiana, the romantic-minded girl who falls in love with an older man. Instead of just hoping, however, I decided to share with James my desire to move into roles of real substance. I was pleased to find this courage in myself, and even happier when James cast me in the part.

In the story, Tatiana falls for the worldly Eugene Onegin, but Onegin rejects her. After fighting a duel and killing a man, Onegin leaves the country. Years later he returns to find Tatiana married and realizes his mistake in turning away her love. Tatiana must choose between her first love and her husband. John Cranko's choreography for the ballet is not rigidly classical in style. The pas de deux were very physical, requiring a lot of upper-body strength. There were a lot of throws and lifts by my partner, and I had to both hang on and resist with my arms and upper back, using my torso as counterbalance. The dancing had to be daring as I brought out the character's tempestuous feelings. Emotional suffering is not pretty; instead of always looking light and beautiful, I had to be real.

At the end of one rehearsal, I had a sore neck and arms. Going home, I complained to Che that I didn't know if I was staying true to the character. *Should I be more understated? Was I acting too young?* Many questions tormented me. Che said, "Chan, don't try to be Tatiana. You have to believe when you're dancing that you *are* Tatiana. That Tatiana is you. Don't try to be her because then you're still someone else just pretending. If you believe that you are this person, if you put yourself into her fate, then you become her. And anything you do will be right."

Che's words gave me the confidence to become Tatiana. In the end, the role was a turning point; I found the power to move beyond the steps, to not merely dance the part but to become it. This was the direction I needed to go if my artistry was to mature. And after *Onegin*, going back to ballets such as *Swan Lake* and *Sleeping Beauty*, I found new ways to imbue them with a deeper meaning, renewing my love for dance when I might have started to grow stale.

A little more than a month later, Che and I ushered in the new year of 1997 by opening a bottle of champagne. Holidays could be a lonely time for me, since they emphasized the fact that I had no close relatives living in Toronto, but we always tried to make the best of them. On this New Year's Eve I was feeling fine; after all, I had just danced a successful and challenging season. I was twenty-seven years old, and Che and I had been engaged for eight years. Suddenly I said to him, "Maybe we should get married this year."

And so we did. The wedding, on August 29, was held at the Rosedale Golf Club with 125 guests. It was a beautiful event that two of my close friends had generously taken charge of planning, for I had turned out to be quite naive about just how much effort a wedding takes. Indeed, they were so helpful that I did not have to take a single day off from the National's dance schedule. Nor did I take time off afterwards; it would be two years before Che and I took our honeymoon, a week in Honolulu before going on to a teaching stint in Japan. Once again, we managed to do things our way, in our own time.

Cutting our wedding cake. I wear a traditional Chinese red silk gown, the color of happiness.

If *Onegin* was the turning point, it led to other exciting roles, culminating in John Cranko's version of *Romeo and Juliet*. I was cast to play opposite Rex Harrington as Romeo. Rex was in demand by companies all over the world for his fine partnering skills. I felt a little intimidated because he had danced the ballet with so many great ballerinas. Even though my acting ability had come a long way, I still wasn't confident that I could unleash the necessary emotions for such a deeply tragic role. During rehearsals, Rex kept telling me to move bigger, to trust him, to expand my gestures. I also spent one weekend working with Veronica Tennant, who had been a brilliantly dramatic Juliet during her own career. Veronica didn't impose her own view of the character, but helped me to shape the role for myself. We especially worked on the scene where Juliet wakes up in the tomb, sees Romeo and is overjoyed until she realizes that he is dead. I had never played a more extreme or sorrowful moment, and I had to work hard to lower my emotional barriers to achieve full self-expression.

*Right after our
wedding ceremony –
we are finally official!*

My debut came in February 1998. Performing the role was more emotionally exhausting than it was physically tiring, but it was also an exhilarating experience. Dancing with Rex at this stage in my career allowed me to more fully reach my potential. After the final curtain call, Rex turned to me and said, "Thank you. I learned so much." We hugged for a long time, and all along I was thinking, "What *you* have taught *me*, I'll never forget." From then on I was sure of the importance of a good partner with whom I could emotionally connect.

I was so pleased to wake the next morning and read the review in the Globe and Mail. The critic noted that many of my previous roles demanded "technical brilliance" as much as they did dramatic ability. But here she called me "an intensely dramatic ballerina who is able to telegraph even the smallest detail of emotional change with her wonderfully expressive face and body. Her complex heroine was forced by circumstance to change almost overnight and leave behind the impetuousness of youth for the steel resolve of adulthood."

For the moment, at least, I was happy.

⟶⟵

A new dance-related pursuit occurred because for years Che had listened to me complaining about pointe shoes. Like most professional dancers, I went through four or five pairs a week during the ten months of the year I was dancing, and rarely was I satisfied. Too often there was a long waiting period before the shoemaker could fill an order, and when the shoes finally arrived it sometimes turned out that they were somehow wrong. The vamp, or top, might be too high, or the shoes might break down too quickly, or they simply might not be consistent from pair to pair. For female dancers especially, finding and getting a continuous supply of the right shoes was a constant problem.

As a teacher, Che himself had often noticed students coming to class with pointe shoes that weren't right for their feet. Either they were as stiff as bricks or they were too soft to offer proper support. When he suggested that they get better shoes, the dancers often explained that

A moment when time stood still; not seeing Paris (Ryan Boorne, left) while looking into the eyes of Romeo (Rex Harrington).

they couldn't afford to, since a pair of pointe shoes can cost more than seventy dollars. To make them last longer, women dancers would use wood shellac inside them, while the men would tape up the ends of their soft slippers with duct tape.

And so one day, Che began to do some drawings of shoes. He had always been interested in design and had recently found out that one of his old classmates in China was now heading a shoe factory. Che had his friend make up some prototype samples and I became his first guinea pig, trying them in class and offering feedback. I gave pairs to other dancers to get their responses. Che took our suggestions and went back to the design table.

Dancers (clockwise from bottom right) Luminita, Ryan, Julie, and Avi showing off various styles of Principal Shoes.

Finally, after a year of trials, Che felt satisfied that he could produce dance shoes that were less expensive but of high quality. We named the company Principal Dance Supplies and went into business. At first we sold the shoes only to professional dancers and other dancers who knew us, but after six months we began to sell them through dance retailers, choosing one reputable store in each major city in Canada. A year later we began to sell them in a few American stores, and after that we began to ship some orders to Japan. Before long we were selling three different styles of pointe shoes, soft ballet slippers, and character shoes. We also collaborated with many designers and began to custom make dance boots for specific productions. By keeping our expenses low — for example, instead of advertising, we rely on word of mouth — we have been able to make the company profitable. A percentage of the profits are donated to the National Ballet's Build-a-Ballet Fund, which commissions new works. We also donate a Principal Shoes Scholarship, to be awarded at festivals and schools across the country. For Che and me both, running a small company has been a constant learning process and a way for us to give something back to the dance community that has been so supportive of us.

❦

It wasn't long after *Romeo and Juliet* that I needed another challenge, another goal to motivate myself and give my dancing purpose. This time it was *The Taming of the Shrew*, the John Cranko ballet based on the Shakespeare play, in which Petruchio marries and then must "tame" the wild and headstrong Kate to make her into a good wife. For several years I had performed the ballet's secondary role of Bianca, the sweet younger sister of Kate, a pretty role but one without much depth. Now with *Shrew* returning to the repertoire, I wanted a chance to dance the lead role of Kate the "shrew," even though I knew that the character would be a real stretch for me.

During a meeting with James Kudelka, I told him how important it was for me to move out of secondary roles and into roles of real substance.

The filming of Four Seasons with James Kudelka (between me and the camera) and Rex Harrington.

Just because I was good at roles like Bianca did not mean I wanted to continue performing them. "Sometimes," I said, "I feel like I'm being punished for doing a good job." James appeared shocked; he had assumed that I would be happy in roles for which I was always praised.

But he listened to my concerns and cast me as Kate opposite Johan Persson. During the first few rehearsals I had trouble convincing even myself that I was making a good Kate. Every time I looked in the mirror, the image I saw was not the cunning, rude, unladylike Kate, but instead a delicate ballerina. I had to let go of everything I had worked so hard to learn and stop being afraid of looking ugly and heavy on my feet. Meanwhile, I had to find a way into the mind of the character. Thinking about her, I felt that I could relate to the fact that, despite her hard exterior, she was very much a woman inside and in need of love.

Throwing myself into the role of this angry, fierce, even bullying woman seemed to affect me in regular life. One day Che told me that I was snapping at him and seemed discontent with everything.

Meanwhile, with the help of Reid Anderson, who had returned to coach the ballet, I was finding Kate. Fortunately, Johan Persson was a brilliant Petruchio. Even when he was making fun of Kate, he did it in such a gentle and affectionate way that I could always believe that there was good in this man.

Some people came to the theater just to see whether or not I could really pull off the role. In the end, I did find my own version of Kate, and my shows went very well. Being so real while on stage demanded a tremendous amount of energy; anger is an exhausting emotion. But I felt that, in playing a role so far from my own natural character, I had proven something important to our audience, and to myself.

I certainly thank James Kudelka for casting me in the kinds of substantial roles that I longed to play. As a choreographer, he created ballets that were very technically and physically challenging, "raising the bar," as he liked to put it. A man with a high sense of artistic integrity, he asked that we dance his works with absolute precision right down to our fingertips. However, his own artistic integrity was always placed first and foremost.

It seems to me that dancing, despite its pressures and difficulties, ought to be a joyful experience. I was lucky to get so much positive feedback and support from Che, my parents, and other members of the dance community. Sometimes, when I went to dance as a guest with another company – always with James' encouragement, for which I was grateful – I would find my enthusiasm and energy rising. Of course I was glad and also proud to be representing the National Ballet of Canada.

REACHING FOR NEW HEIGHTS

In October 2001, I flew from Calgary, where I had just performed with the National Ballet, to Washington Dulles Airport. As soon as I was off the plane, I took a cab to the Kennedy Center to jump into a rehearsal with the Suzanne Farrell Ballet, with whom I was engaged as principal dancer. Our opening was in three days.

After the Kennedy Center season, we began a two-week tour, with perhaps the most important stop being the New Jersey Performing Arts Center. The theater was beautiful, reminiscent of an opera house. Here I was to dance in two Balanchine works, *Scotch Symphony* and *La Sonnambula,* before an audience that would include New York critics coming to see the new company founded by the most famous of Balanchine's leading dancers and inspirations. While I had danced both works at the Kennedy Center and on tour with the company, it would be the first time I would dance both in one show, and Suzanne had asked me whether I thought I could do it. "It'll be hard on my feet but I'll be fine," I said, smiling.

Now retired from dancing, Suzanne had been a principal dancer with the New York City Ballet. It was for this company that George Balanchine, the most brilliant choreographer of the 20th century, created most of his dances. Balanchine had left his native Russia, where he began his career, and eventually settled in the United States, becoming the artistic director of the New York City Ballet on its founding in 1948. His style is called "neoclassical" – a new approach to the traditional movements of dance. Although he died in 1983, his works continue to be performed by companies around the world. Instead of telling a story, most of his ballets are inspired responses to music. The dancing is often fast and light, the steps intricate, and the dancers must have a fine mastery of technique. Instead of being about something like love or youth or loneliness, Balanchine's ballets are about movement itself – "pure beauty," as Balanchine once said. For a dancer they are both a challenge and a joy to perform.

I had not expected to have the opportunity to dance such once-in-a-lifetime repertoire, which also included Jerome Robbins' *Afternoon of a Faun*, a pure indulgence. Nor had I expected ever to work with a dancer I admired as much as I did Suzanne – an admiration born when I had seen her perform in Balanchine's *Mozartiana* on that family trip to New York so many years ago. She had come to the National to stage *Mozartiana* and, although I hadn't originally been selected to work with her, Suzanne chose me for it after watching me dance. After that, Suzanne returned to Canada to stage *Jewels* and asked me to dance the section called "Diamonds," which Balanchine had originally created for her. I felt honored to dance both of these extraordinary roles, and to receive coaching from Suzanne – this was as close as a dancer could come to being directed by Balanchine himself. Her nurturing quality and motivating encouragement had infused me with a renewed sense of love for dance.

And now, here I was in New Jersey. Just a month before, the September 11 World Trade Center tragedy had occurred, and no one had really recovered from the shock and grief of so many deaths. But at

"Take your time; don't rush."   *"Follow through; grow."*   *"Look; reach; aim high."*

Suzanne Farrell coaching me in "Diamonds" from Jewels.

the same time, people felt that life had to go on, and that the positive values of sharing, affection, love, and creativity ought to be celebrated. I was glad to be contributing to the establishment of Suzanne's company, and to be a part of the experience of giving pleasure to the large and appreciative audience. While I was anxious with anticipation, as I still felt at times, I was also glad to find myself feeling more confident than in the past. I had matured as a dancer and a person, and Suzanne's continuing support also contributed to my greater sense of sureness. The next day I couldn't help but be pleased to open the *New York Times* and read of "the merry, sweet-tempered performance of Chan Hon Goh . . . who bears a faint but potent resemblance to Margot Fonteyn." The reviewer felt I brought "a fleeting, old-style perfume to the role of the sylph [in *Scotch Symphony*], and the lyrical quality of her dancing and that of the female corps was a special pleasure."

❧

And so my life as a dancer continues. In the morning when I awake, my body resists getting out of bed because of the inevitable pain. It might be a sore neck, or pain in my hips or feet, but something almost always hurts. I think of that first cup of coffee and the pleasures and challenges of the day to come, and I make myself get up. Walking down the long stairway in our house, I feel like I'm a seventy-five-year-old lady.

Sometimes a rehearsal day can be harder than a performance day. It begins with a morning class at the Walter Carsen Centre (our present home), the waterfront building of the National Ballet. I arrive at the studio wearing a sweater and leg warmers over my tights and leotard, and wool socks and down-filled boots over my ballet slippers. By the time I've finished the barre work, my body has warmed up and I have stripped off the extra garments, changing my slippers for pointe shoes in preparation for center work. Even now classes are very important to me. They are a chance to improve each step, to work on my turnout and flexibility, to strive for greater precision, speed, and coordination. Although I am now a principal dancer, the instructor will still come by and correct me. And just as I did as a student, I watch the other dancers, looking for fine qualities from which I can learn.

At the end of class, I have fifteen minutes before first rehearsal, during which I change into a fresh leotard — my first will have been soaked through. Rehearsals are usually an hour long and I may have as many as three before lunch break. In each hour I may work on a different piece — an hour spent on the full-length ballet, and the other hours devoted to shorter works for a mixed program. Rehearsals can be a breeze or a struggle, depending on the ballet and my partner. Although I may feel as if I'm getting nowhere, I have to trust that it always gets better.

Between each rehearsal there is a break of just a few minutes, and I may eat part of a protein bar to keep up my blood-sugar level. For lunch, I grab something to eat in the cafeteria, sitting down with whichever dancers happen to be around. Despite my hunger, I can't eat too much — maybe half a sandwich and the rest of the protein bar— because it is hard to rehearse on a full stomach. Then it's back to the studio, where we may not finish until six-thirty. I rehearse a maximum of six hours in one day. The day can feel very long, but the discoveries

*Che teaching
us in a class
at the National
Ballet's Walter
Carsen Centre.*

made along the way, even the ability to laugh at myself sometimes, make it go faster.

There are other responsibilities to be taken care of, and any hours in which I am not scheduled to rehearse get quickly filled up. I might have interviews with newspaper, magazine, or television journalists, or a photo shoot. Or I might have a costume fitting, which can take up to an hour if it's for a new work and the designer is still working things out. For a ballet already in the repertoire, it's a matter of altering a costume to fit me (principal dancers share costumes because they are so costly). Costumes can make a dancer look better on stage, but they can also be a problem. Sometimes the way they are cut or the kind of fabric chosen can hinder a dancer. Sometimes it's the sheer weight of the thing – all the layers of tulle in a tutu, along with the intricate beadwork and other decoration. But our talented wardrobe staff help make me as comfortable as they can.

If there's time, I will book myself a massage or a physiotherapy session. Even if I am injury-free, I try to have massages every week to stay in good condition. If anything feels out of line – my neck won't turn through its full range, or my foot won't point fully – I go to the physiotherapist before the problem gets worse. I have learned to listen to my body and react to any warning signs, even when the reason for the pain is not easy to figure out.

Occasionally in the evening there is an event for supporters of the ballet. While I am not required to attend, I like to meet the people who support our company and come to see me in virtually every role I perform.

If there are no other obligations, I gladly go home to Che and Daly. Not only am I exhausted, I am also famished. Che and I eat in or, if neither of us has the energy to cook, we go to a restaurant. We hardly ever talk about ballet; it is nice to feel that I am in the real world for a few hours. Later at home, we take care of necessities – answering messages, opening the mail, doing the laundry, and dealing with our shoe business. Or I might just be so tired that I'll flop in front of the TV and let everything wait for another day. Che tries not to talk to me about business after ten o'clock. Otherwise, it takes me a long time to stop my thoughts from racing. And sleep is a treasured necessity.

A performance day is different. All my energy is focused on the show. I have the morning to myself, and I'll get to the theater around midday to take a class and rehearse (not more than two hours on a performance day). Then comes the important task of deciding which pair of pointe shoes to wear for the performance. I will have several pairs that have been worked in during class, and now must decide which feel best on my feet that day. Each pair of pointe shoes is used for only one performance, and sometimes I go through three pairs a show.

Looking beyond, ready for the future.

I might have a massage or a physiotherapy session. Then I'll have lunch and won't eat another meal until after the show.

Whenever possible, I try to go home and take a nap before I'm due at the theater for an evening performance, not just to refresh myself but also to achieve calm. Two hours before curtain, I arrive at the Hummingbird Centre. In the dressing room, which I share with two other dancers, I begin to apply my makeup and do my hair. My dressing room is well stocked with chocolates, protein bars, cookies, and water.

After a short warm-up in the rehearsal studio, I put on my pointe shoes. Over the loudspeaker comes the announcement: five-minute call. I put on my costume with the help of my dresser. When the onstage call is announced, I take my place, either on the stage or in the wings waiting for my entrance.

Two and a half hours later, the final curtain comes down. Depending on the ballet and my mood, I may be exhausted, emotional, pleased, or critical of my own performance. There are flowers from fans and from Che, who sends me a bouquet for each of my performances, wherever I dance. The director and the coach wait in the wings to offer their comments.

In the dressing room, the dresser helps me out of my costume. I always like it when my partner comes to say goodbye before he leaves. Almost before I am changed, the audience members with permission – friends, family, and sometimes regular ballet-goers I have come to know – arrive backstage. When finally I leave the theater, there may be fans waiting for autographs.

At last the evening is over. It is late and Che and I go in search of a place to eat. We relax and wind down, and when we get home I often take a bath. And then, once again, it's sleep – for tomorrow I have to dance again.

✐

As a child, I once overheard a friend of my parents ask about my future: "Is Chan going to be a dancer?"

*"Diamonds"
in* Jewels: *hearing the applause and feeling that I am the thankful one.*

My father answered, "No, we don't want her to be. Life is too hard for a dancer."

Now that I am a dancer, I can understand better my parents' reservations about my following their own career. Ballet takes so much time and dedication that it is difficult to pursue other interests or fields of education. A dancer spends years learning a kind of "language" that is understood only in the dance world. There is no guarantee – indeed, the odds are against it – that as a dancer you will succeed enough to satisfy your ambitions. And if you do, it means unceasing work to maintain and improve your technique, keep in shape, learn new roles.

The career is not usually well-paying and it is short-lived. Dancers usually retire in their late thirties or early forties, when people in other professions are still building their careers. The glamorous aspects – interviews, your photograph in the newspapers, curtain-call bravos, and roses – soon lose some of their shine.

And yet, knowing all this, my love and passion for the art still answers "Yes" a hundred times over to the question of whether I am glad to be a dancer. What ballet will I be cast in next? How can I deepen my interpretations of the great roles in the repertoire? Where will I next appear as a guest artist, working for the first time with other talented directors and dancers? The adventure of my dancing life continues.

A while ago I was receiving a massage to relax my muscles, when the therapist said to me, "Chan, it seems that you're always in a hurry to get some place. What about the process. What about *now?*" I thought, *Yes, I have been focused on reaching one goal and then the next. I have not valued the process, the experience, enough.* So now I tell myself to enjoy each moment for its own sake. The class. The rehearsal. The second before leaping onto the stage before the audience. And then the quiet time at home again.

Still, I can't help looking forward to the next goal, the next challenge. It's a simple truth of my character. For me, to reach for new heights is to be alive.

ACKNOWLEDGMENTS

CHAN HON GOH

First and foremost I have to thank Avie Bennett, without whose guidance and support this book would not exist. And to Kathy Lowinger, for her vision and encouragement.

I would like to thank the following for their assistance and confidence in me: Alison Armitage, Lida Baday, Dorinda Chiang, Che Chun, Jonathon Lovat Dickson, Julia Drake, Sonya Dunn, Cary Fagan, Nicole Roy Leonard, Sally Szuster, Sharon Vanderlinde. Valerie Wilder, Max Wyman, and the National Ballet of Canada.

CARY FAGAN

I want to thank Chan Hon Goh for sharing her experiences with me and for her willingness to go beneath the surface. Choo Chiat and Lin Yee Goh recalled their own dramatic lives and gave me a vivid sense of their daughter Chan as a child. Showing me about their dance school in Vancouver, I could easily feel the pride they continue to take in their young dancers. Thanks also to Kathy Lowinger for believing that I was the right person to help tell this story.

Among the useful books that I consulted, I wish to note especially the following: Anatole Chujoy and P.W. Manchester, *The Dance Encyclopedia*; Mary Clarke and Clement Crisp, *Ballet: an Illustrated History* and *The Ballet Goers' Guide*; Suzanne Farrell, *Holding On To The Air*; Mary Kerner, *Barefoot to Balanchine: How to Watch Dance*; and James Neufeld, *The Power To Rise: The Story of The National Ballet of Canada*.

PHOTO CREDITS

Joseph Ciancio: 87; Courtesy of the Goh family: 11, 14, 15, 16, 21, 22, 27, 30, 31, 42, 48, 54, 56, 61, 64, 69, 75, 76, 108, 118, 121, 132, 133; Andrew Oxenham: 6, 44, 96, 97, 98–99, 125, 149; Lydia Pawelak: 8, 89, 92, 128, 134; Johan Persson: 18, 130; David Street: 50, 78, 93, 103; Cylla von Tiedemann: 1, 12, 25, 34, 40, 58, 70, 82, 88, 90, 91, 94, 95, 100, 112, 114, 122, 136, 138, 140, 143, 146; Bruce Zinger: 145.